The Pragmatics of Discourse Anaphora in English

Topics in English Linguistics 14

Editor

Herman Wekker

Mouton de Gruyter
Berlin · New York

The Pragmatics of Discourse Anaphora in English

Evidence from Conversational Repair

Ronald Geluykens

Mouton de Gruyter
Berlin · New York 1994

Mouton de Gruyter (formerly Mouton, The Hague)
is a Division of Walter de Gruyter & Co., Berlin.

⊗ Printed on acid-free paper which falls within the guidelines of the
ANSI to ensure permanence and durability.

Library of Congress Cataloging-in-Publication Data

Geluykens, Ronald.
   The pragmatics of discourse anaphora in English : evi-
dence from conversational repair / Ronald Geluykens.
      p.   cm. − (Topics in English linguistics ; 14)
   Revision of the author's thesis (Ph. D) − Cambridge.
   Includes bibliographical references and indexes.
   ISBN 3-11-013416-0 (cloth : acid-free)
   1. English language − Anaphora,   2. English language −
Discourse analysis.   3. English language − Spoken English.
4. Conversation.   5. Pragmatics.   I. Title.   II. Series.
PE1398.A52G45   1994
425 − dc20   94-12629
                                                          CIP

Die Deutsche Bibliothek − Cataloging-in-Publication Data

Geluykens, Ronald:
The pragmatics of discourse anaphora in English : evidence
from conversational repair / by Ronald Geluykens. − Berlin ;
New York : Mouton de Gruyter, 1994
(Topics in English linguistics ; 14)
Zugl.: Cambridge, Univ., Diss.
ISBN 3-11-013416-0
NE: GT

Printing: Gerike GmbH, Berlin. Binding: Lüderitz & Bauer, Berlin.
Printed in Germany.

Preface

This study, which is a revised version of my Cambridge Ph.D., could not have been written without the help of several people, and I want to acknowledge my indebtedness to them here. First of all, I am extremely grateful to my Ph.D. supervisor, Steve Levinson, for the continuing support he has given me thoughout the period in which this study was conceived.

My gratitude also goes to my Ph.D. examiners, Gillian Brown and Geoffrey Leech, for their many comments and suggestions. I am also indebted to Sidney Greenbaum, not only for giving me access to that invaluable database, the Survey of English Usage, but also for his continuing support and detailed comments on earlier versions. My sincere thanks also go to Louis Goossens and to René Collier for their very detailed comments on earlier drafts of this study. I should also mention the comments from Peter Matthews, Sandy Thompson and Barbara Fox. Finally, I ought to acknowledge the suggestions from my series editors, Herman Wekker and Jan Svartvik.

Earlier versions of parts of this study were presented at the Second Functional Grammar Conference (University of Antwerp, September 1986; cf. Geluykens 1987a), at the 25th Regional Meeting of the Chicago Linguistic Society (University of Chicago, April 1989; cf. Geluykens 1989a), and at the Fourth International Functional Grammar Conference (University of Copenhagen, June 1990). Oral versions were also presented at the University of Nottingham (January 1987), University College London (June 1987), the Max Planck Institut für Psycholinguistik, Nijmegen (February 1989), the University of California at Santa Barbara (June 1989), the University of Oxford (January 1990), and the University of Reading (March 1990). I am grateful to all the comments received on these preliminary versions from the people attending those presentations, and must apologize for not mentioning them all in person. The people mentioned above are, of course, not to be held responsible for any remaining errors; these are entirely my own responsibility.

I am very grateful to Trinity College, Cambridge, for giving me the opportunity to carry out this piece of research, by offering me an External Research Studentship, and for providing all the facilities required; I am likewise grateful to The Queen's College, Oxford, for offering me a Junior Research Fellowship in Linguistics, which enabled me to finish the writing of this study in a serene manner. My sincere thanks go to both colleges for offering me the opportunity to work in a stimulating academic environment. Finally, I have to thank the Belgian National Fund for Scientific Research (NFWO) and the University of Antwerp (UFSIA) for offering me the financial and material support, respectively, to finish this study.

Table of contents

Chapter 1

Introduction

1.1. General goals and scope

This study deals with the behaviour of certain referential forms in English conversational discourse. More particularly, it deals with the factors governing the speaker's choice between, on the one hand, a fully lexical NP and, on the other hand, a pronominalized form. Since the choice between the two forms will depend to a large extent on the "anchoring" of the referential form in the discourse context, in other words on its having some type of antecedent in that context, this study thus deals, on a general level, with the factors underlying certain types of discourse anaphora.

We use the term discourse anaphora here as a category distinct from sentential anaphora, to indicate that we will not be concerned here with NPs which are subject to some form of syntactic "binding" within the sentence in which they appear (see Reinhart 1983). The NPs which interest us are governed not by syntactic conditions, but by pragmatic principles operating on the discourse level. To illustrate the difference between the two types of NP, consider (1) and (2) below:

(1) *John₁ said that John₂ would come.*

(2) *John₁ and Bill₂ came in. John₁ said that he would come.*

Whereas the criteria which force a non-coreferential reading for the two occurrences of *John* in (1) are syntactic in nature, those generating a (likely) coreferential reading of the two occurrences of *John* in (2) are not. First of all, there are no strict rules for the interpretation of (2); secondly, the principles underlying the coreference behaviour of (2) are of a contextual, pragmatic nature, determined by the discourse context created by the first sentence of (2). We will only be concerned here with NPs of the latter type.

The behaviour of discourse anaphors, we will argue in the remainder of this study, can be explained in terms of two general pragmatic principles, which we will label the Economy principle (or E-principle) and the Clarity principle (or C-principle), respectively (see chapter 2 for a full discussion). These principles, which are ultimately based on Grice's (1975) Quantity maxims, govern not only the choice between pronominal form and full NP, but lie at the basis of much of what we will label, following Chafe (1987), "information flow" in conversation, and more particularly those aspects relating to the realization of information in discourse. The data presented in this study show that these principles indeed exist, that they can be used as general explanatory parameters for the behaviour of referential forms, and that there is a tension between the two principles which sometimes gives rise to certain trouble spots in production.

It is these trouble spots that we will be concerned with in particular, as they provide evidence for the tension existing between the E- and C-principles. The trouble spots often give rise to a certain type of conversational "repair" (Schegloff—Jefferson—Sacks 1977), whereby one type of referential form (in this case a pronominal) is replaced by another (in this case mostly a full NP). The repairs under investigation here are not concerned with "errors" in the strict sense, but rather have to do with the felicitousness, or appropriateness, of use of certain referential expressions; Levelt (1989) labels these repairs "appropriateness repairs" (but we will argue further on that this label is not a very apt one). As a first indication of the process concerned, consider (3):

(3)   A: *I'm not sure whether he will come tomorrow.*
        B: *who is that you're talking about?*
        A: *John I mean.*

In this exchange, use of the pronominal *he* in the first turn gives rise to the initiation of a repair by B in the second turn; in the third turn, speaker A self-repairs his original utterance by substituting the lexical NP *John* for the original pronominal form. We will go into the nature of conversational repair in more detail in chapter 2.

From the point of view of information flow, we will argue that the existence of trouble spots such as the one in (3) above are, ultimately, due to the pragmatic status of the referential form involved. This status will depend to a large extent on the relationship between the form and the preceding discourse context, more particularly on the type of antecedent the form has in that context. The status of the referential form can be expressed in terms of what is usually labelled in the literature "givenness-newness", labels which we will replace, for reasons we will discuss in chapter 2, with the concept of Recoverability (see also Geluykens 1988a, 1992, 1993). The repair is thus generated by the existence of a tension between two pragmatic principles, which can be translated into the NP in question having a problematic recoverability status with regard to the preceding discourse record. This study thus also tries to shed some new light on the concept of "givenness" through the empirical analysis of conversational data.

The preceding paragraphs have already outlined some of the main objectives of this study. First of all, it is an attempt to contribute to pragmatic theory, by providing empirical evidence for certain general pragmatic principles operating in conversational discourse. Secondly, by using certain conversation-analytic concepts, we do not only hope to show that CA methodology is a useful tool for the empirical study of pragmatics, but we also want to contribute to the study of conversational repair in CA. Thirdly, this study deals with certain aspects of the discourse-analytic concept of information flow; it provides some empirical evidence for the claim that previous accounts of "givenness" in the literature are less than fully satisfactory for the analysis of conversational discourse. In a way, this study thus attempts to combine elements of DA and CA methodology (see also the discussion in Geluykens (1992); we will return to this in section 1.2.

The study also raises some general issues about the nature of conversational discourse. First of all, our data show that not only the establishing of reference in conversation (cf. Geluykens 1988b), but also the subsequent tracking of those referents which have been introduced (cf. also Geluykens 1989a), is a collaborative process, a joint effort between speaker and hearer. The speaker (who we will refer to with the masculine *he* , purely for the sake of convenience), as we hope to show, relies heavily on hearer-feedback when building up his part of the discourse; this feedback can be both explicit (verbal or non-verbal) and implicit. One could even argue that the terms "speaker" and "hearer" (to which we will stick throughout this study, for convenience' sake) are rather unfortunate, as they suggest an "active" and "passive" participant, whereas the interactional reality is rather different. We will return to this in due course. Secondly, our data also show that conversation is not organized in a strictly linear way, but that it is hierarchically organized. A purely linear, quantitative approach to information flow in conversation would thus be inappropriate.

Apart from the goals outlined above, there are a number of other points which this study tackles. First of all, our data raise some important questions about the relationship between discourse (or, more particularly, conversation) and syntax. To illustrate this point (to which we will return in detail later on), consider (4):

(4)   *He said he would come, John I mean.*

This is an instance of repair of the type also exemplified by (3) above, this time with speaker-initiation rather than hearer-initiation. At the same time, on a syntactic level, the string *He said he would come, John* could be regarded as a construction in its own right, more particularly the construction which is usually labelled "right-dislocation" in the literature (following Ross 1967, 1986; henceforth RD). The structure in (4) could thus both be regarded as the reflection of a certain interactional repair-process and as a grammatical construction; this raises questions about the relationship between discourse and grammar (or, more generally, between communicative function and linguistic form), to which we will return in due course (chapter 6).

Although this study focuses mainly on the interactional aspects of conversational discourse, it is clear that our findings also have some implications for a theory of language production, and hence are of interest to psycholinguistics. Reasons of space and scope do not permit us to go into these in any great detail, but certain aspects will be touched upon in passing.

Finally, we ought to point out that this study deals in some detail with prosodic aspects of conversation. Prosody is a factor which is all too often ignored, or not given enough attention, in the discourse-analytic literature; we firmly believe that it is one of the factors which ought to be incorporated in any theory of pragmatics. We will make use of Crystal's (1969) system of prosodic analysis (see chapter 2 for details).

1.2. A note on methodology

It should be clear from the preceding section that our methodology is a resolutely empirical one. Despite the philosophical tradition which lies at the basis of many developments in pragmatics (e.g. speech act theory), we believe that the pragmatic principles underlying verbal interaction can only be unravelled through meticulous examination of naturally occurring data. Our analysis is corpus-based, relying on a large corpus (350,000 words) of, mostly spontaneous, conversational discourse (both face-to-face and telephone conversations are included; cf. section 2.4).

The methodology employed here is a mixture of the methodologies of two schools of thought which are both concerned with the analysis of discourse and which, following Levinson (1983), we will label Conversation Analysis (DA) and Discourse Analysis (CA), respectively. This is not the place to go into an in-depth discussion of both schools; we refer the reader to the recent studies by Levinson (1983; chapter 6) and Brown—Yule (1983), respectively. In what follows, we will merely highlight the differences between the two schools which are relevant to our analysis, and their respective shortcomings. We will argue in favour of a synthesis between DA and CA; such a synthesis has already proved useful in a different context (cf. Geluykens 1992).

As far as DA is concerned, a lot of the work on information flow is especially useful for our purposes. In this type of work, discourse is viewed mainly as the transmission of information from a speaker (writer) to a hearer (reader), and certain constraints or discourse "rules" can be formulated to explain why discourse information is structured the way it is. So, for instance, a tendency can be noted for "given" information to be pronominalized, and for "new" information to be presented as a (usually indefinite) lexical NP.

There are, however, certain problems with the DA approach, which we will briefly summarize here. First of all, DA tends to focus on the information flow aspect of discourse to the exclusion of all other aspects. This would suggest that the main, if not only, function of language is referring to entities and predicating over the entities referred to. As Foley—Van Valin (1984) rightly point out, however, "referring-and-predicating is only one of the socially constituted functions of language (...). Hence in talking about communication, we do not mean this narrow sense but rather a concept encompassing a wide variety of speech events found in society" (Foley—Van Valin 1984: 8). Although the main focus of attention in this study is indeed on the process of "reference" in discourse, it should be kept in mind that this referring, especially in conversational discourse, always occurs in a social and interactional context, and thus has a clear interactive dimension which should not be ignored (part of the purpose of this study is in fact to make precisely this point).

A second, and related, point concerns the nature of the data DA focuses on. Many DA studies are mainly concerned with narrative discourse (e.g. Givón 1983, to name an exponent to which we will return several times; there are of course many exceptions, e.g. Coulthard 1977, Sinclair—Coulthard 1975, Stubbs 1983). Far too little attention is paid to conversational discourse, which is after all the most widespread type of discourse, and is also the least constrained, in the sense of not being very limited by social factors such as setting and the like. This concentration on narrative is easy to understand, as narrative is the "simplest" form of discourse, in the sense of it being the most linear, and one of the least interactive, types of discourse. We think that it would be dangerous to extrapolate the findings on narrative discourse directly to deal with conversational discourse. As we will attempt to show in our analyses, a simple linear, quantitative approach to information flow in conversation is unsatisfactory, since there are a lot of interactional factors which have to be taken into account.

The third and final drawback about a lot of DA work on information flow is that it abounds with theoretical apparatus which is insufficiently operational, that is to say not defined rigorously enough to be useful for tackling real conversational data. We will return to this in some detail in section 2.3, where we will also formulate an alternative proposal.

As far as CA work is concerned, the main criticism that can be aimed at it, from a linguist's point of view, is that it does not pay enough attention to aspects of linguistic structure (once again, there are exceptions, most notably the work of Schegloff; cf. Schegloff 1979, 1987). This lack of attention is easily understood, given the historical origins of CA, but it is a pity, as CA can have a lot to contribute to the linguistic-pragmatic study of discourse, as we hope to show in the remainder of this study.

One advantage of CA is that it does pay a lot of attention to the interactional side of discourse. In particular, the concept of repair which lies at the heart of our analysis is a CA one. Although we will make abstraction of a lot of social factors such as conversational settings and relations between participants, the turn-taking system (Sacks—Schegloff—Jefferson 1974) is prominent in our analysis.

Another advantage of CA is the strict empirical approach, which shows among other things in the absence of too much apriori apparatus. This is a methodology we will also adhere to in this study.

It remains for us to define what exactly we mean by "conversation"; we will take over Levinson's (1983) definition of conversation as "that familiar predominant kind of talk in which two or more participants freely alternate in speaking, which generally occurs outside specific institutional settings like religious services, law courts, classrooms and the like" (Levinson 1983: 284).

We should note that this is a relatively narrow definition; in fact, some of the conversations employed as data in this study do not really belong in this category, as some of the texts used (all data are taken from the Survey of English Usage) are from interview situations (this is only a small minority of the database, however).

1.3. Outline of the analysis

Before embarking on the analysis itself, it might be worthwhile to sketch briefly the organization of this study. In the following chapter, we develop the theoretical framework needed for the empirical analysis in later chapters.

The empirical analysis itself starts with chapter 3. The interactional discussion of how the pragmatic principles give rise to anaphor-repairs is organized according to the main types of repair. Chapter 3 deals with instances of other-initiated self-repair; chapter 4 is concerned with self-initiated self-repair. Chapter 7 deals with (mostly other-initiated) other-repairs.

In chapter 5, we will discuss the informational status of the repair-items, i.e. the relationship between the original pronominal referential form and the preceding context. Chapter 6 deals with the relationship between self-repair and the syntactic construction "right-dislocation".

Chapters 8 and 9 conclude the empirical analysis, and deal with certain types of repair which have been left out of the picture in the previous chapters. It will be argued that the same pragmatic principles can be invoked to explain these repairs, and that they are indirect evidence for the functional tendencies claimed in previous chapters.

In chapter 10, finally, we will summarize the main arguments of this study, draw some general conclusions from them, and place them in a broader perspective.

Chapter 2

Theoretical framework

2.1. Pragmatic principles in conversational discourse

2.1.1. The cooperative principle (Grice 1975)

This study tries to show, among other things, that the establishing of discourse anaphora, i.e. the process whereby an element picks up its reference through an item in the previous context, is an interactional process depending on speaker-hearer collaboration. It will also attempt to show that some general conversational principles, originating in Grice's (1975) conversational maxims, can have explanatory value in accounting for the behaviour of discourse anaphors. We will show that there is a tension between two conversational principles which are, as it were, in competition, and that this tension may result in conversational repair (Schegloff et al. 1977).

Let us start from Grice's (1975) cooperative principle, which is formulated as follows (Grice 1975: 45):

(5)   Make your contribution such as is required, at the stage at which it
        occurs, by the accepted purpose or direction of the talk exchange in
        which you are engaged.

The cooperative principle can be translated into a number of maxims, some of which are essential to our thesis, more particularly those which have a direct impact on the linguistic realization of referential elements in discourse, viz. Quantity and Manner. The two quantity maxims are characterized as follows by Grice:

(6)   Quantity 1:   make your contribution as informative as is
                      required for the current purposes of the exchange;
        Quantity 2:   do not make your contribution more informative
                      than is required. (Grice 1975)

It is clear that these two maxims make different predictions as to what the speaker should do to effect efficient communication. Whereas Q1 would predict that the speaker has to give as much information as he possibly can, Q2 predicts that he has to supply infomation in as economical a way as he possibly can. This apparent contradiction is also present in the Manner maxim ("be perspicuous"), which is broken down into four sub-maxims:

(7)   (i)   M1: avoid obscurity;
         (ii)   M2: avoid ambiguity;
         (iii)   M3: be brief;
         (iv)   M4: be orderly. (Grice 1975)

Whereas M1 and M2 would suggest that, in order to avoid obscurity and ambiguity, the speaker should opt for maximally clear (and thus probably more complex) linguistic expressions, M3 suggests that economy of expression should be a prime consideration. There is thus, at the very least, an area of tension between some of the maxims.

2.1.2. Q-based and R-based implicatures (Horn 1985)

We are not the first to note this clash between Gricean principles: Levinson (1987, 1988), for instance, has also pointed out that there are potential clashes between some of the maxims (see section 2.1.3). Levinson is in turn influenced by Horn (1985), who suggests that all that is necessary to replace Grice's maxims (apart from Quality) are two different principles:

(8)   The Q-principle: make your contribution sufficient
             ("say as much as you can");
         The R-principle: make your contribution necessary
             ("say no more than you must").

The synthesis or resolution of these two antitheses is summarized by Horn as follows, by invoking the notion of "markedness":

> The use of a marked (relatively complex and/or prolix) expression when a corresponding unmarked (simpler, less 'effortful') alternate expression is available tends to be interpreted as conveying a marked message (one

which the unmarked alternative would not or could not have conveyed).
(Horn 1985: 22)

What this boils down to is the following. Whenever a speaker has the choice between two alternate expressions to express the same message, the R-principle will dictate that he ought to use the unmarked alternative. When the speaker does use the marked alternative, this will implicate (through the Q-principle) some aspect of meaning which the unmarked form could not have conveyed.

2.1.3. Q-, I-, and Q/M-principles (Levinson 1987, 1988)

Levinson has developed a set of principles which are similar to Horn's (1985). The first principle, deriving from the first Quantity maxim, is actually less relevant for our purposes, but we mention it here for completeness' sake:

(9)   Q-principle

> *Speaker's Maxim:* Do not provide a statement that is
> informationally weaker than your knowledge of the world allows,
> unless providing a stronger statement would contravene the I-
> principle.
> *Recipient's Corollary:* Take it that the speaker made the strongest
> statement consistent with what he knows. (Levinson 1988: 401)

In other words, whenever a speaker uses a weaker statement where he could have used a stronger one (on a Horn-scale, e.g. the *some-all* scale below), this will Q-implicate that the stronger one does not hold. This principle is needed to explain implicatures of the kind expressed by (10):

(10)   (a)   *Some of the students showed.*
         (b)   *All of the students showed.*

Utterance (6a) Q-implicates that utterance (6b) does not hold, since use of the informationally weaker *some* where the speaker could have used the stronger *all* would contradict the Q-principle.
    More relevant to our purposes is what Levinson (see also Atlas—Levinson 1981) labels the Informativeness (or I-)principle, the relevant parts of which are summarized in (11) below:

(11)   I-Principle
Speaker's Maxim (the Maxim of Minimization)
'Say as little as necessary', i.e. produce the minimal linguistic
information sufficient to achieve your communicational ends
(bearing the Q-principle in mind).
Recipient's Corollary (the Enrichment Rule)
Amplify the informational content of the speaker's utterance, by
finding the most SPECIFIC interpretation, up to what you judge
to be the speaker's m-intended point.
Specifically:
  (a)   (...)
  (b)   (...)
  (c)   Avoid interpretations that multiply entities referred to
        (assume referential parsimony); specifically, *prefer
        coreferential readings of reduced NPs* (pronouns or
        zeros). (Levinson 1988: 402; my emphasis)

It is clear that the I-principle is essentially nothing more than a
detailed reformulation of Horn's (1985) R-principle, and also
originates in Grice's second Quantity maxim. The attraction of this
reformulation is that it distinguishes between the speaker's and
hearer's point of view. Note also that the potential relevance of this
principle for dealing with anaphora is noted (and empirically
validated in Levinson 1987, 1988).

Levinson admits to the existence of an antithetical principle (cf.
Horn's Q-principle), the implicatures from which he re-labels "Q/M-
implicatures", to indicate that they are related to the maxim of Manner
as well as Quantity. Indeed, as he rightly points out, the use of a
more prolix or marked expression "has nothing to do with quantity of
information, the paired expressions being assumed to be
synonymous; rather, it has to do with surface form, and these
implicatures are thus properly attributed to the maxim of Manner"
(Levinson 1988: 409). He has to admit, however, that Quantity also
enters the equation, hence the rather awkward label. In fact, we will
conflate Quantity and Manner into a single set of principles later on.

As a way of resolving the potential clashes between the three
different types of implicature, Levinson suggests the following
resolution scheme:

(12)   (i)   Genuine Q-implicatures from tight contrast sets of equally
               brief, equally lexicalized linguistic expressions 'about' the
               same semantic relations, take precedence over I-implicatures

(ii)   in all other cases the I-principle induces stereotypical
        specific interpretations, UNLESS:

(iii)   there are two (or more) available expressions of the same
        sense, one of which is unmarked and the other marked
        in form. In that case, the unmarked form carries the I-
        implicatures as usual, but the use of the marked form
        Q/M-implicates the non-applicability of the pertinent I-
        implicatures. (Levinson 1988: 409)

This, of course, bears a strong resemblance to the resolution scheme
suggested by Horn (1985) for his Q- and R-implicatures.

2.1.4. The textual rhetoric (Leech 1983)

In Leech (1983), a pragmatic theory is proposed which contains,
apart from Grice's original maxims, a number of other maxims.
Leech's proposal is worth going into, as it constitutes an attempt at
an explicit theory of linguistic pragmatics based on Gricean
principles.

First of all, Leech distinguishes between what he calls the
Interpersonal rhetoric and the Textual rhetoric. The interpersonal
rhetoric contains, among other things, Grice's cooperative principle.
The Gricean maxims are largely taken over, so we have the original
versions of the Quantity and Manner maxims. On top of that,
however, there is a textual rhetoric, which contains four main
principles, which in their turn can be subdivided into maxims. Those
principles are the Processibility, Clarity, Economy, and Expressivity
principles, respectively.

The Processibility principle dictates that a piece of discourse
should be presented in such a way that it is easy for the hearer to
decode in time (Leech 1983: 64). This is thus tied up with the linear
ordering of the message, and with the assignment of degrees of
prominence to different parts of the message. This principle gives
rise to the Maxims of End-focus and End-weight, which we will not
go into in detail.

The Clarity Principle is of more direct interest to this study. It can
be broken down into a Transparency Maxim and an Ambiguity
Maxim. The latter maxim simply reads "avoid ambiguity" (Leech
1983: 66), but is distinguished from Grice's Manner maxim. Leech
argues that there are two kinds of Clarity, which should not be
confused:

> One kind consists in making unambiguous use of the syntax and phonology of the language in order to construct a clear TEXT. Another type of clarity consists in framing a clear MESSAGE, i.e. a message which is perspicuous or intelligible in the sense of conveying the intended illocutionary goal to the addressee. (Leech 1983: 100)

It is the former type of clarity which is covered by the Clarity Principle outlined above; the latter type of clarity relates to the Manner Maxim.

Another principle which is very relevant to this study is the Economy Principle, which is paraphrased as "be quick and easy" (Leech 1983: 67), and which states that one should reduce the text wherever possible. Leech notes that the Clarity Principle and the Economy Principle are "continually at war" (Leech 1982: 100) with each other, and that a balance has to be struck between, on the one hand, the saving of time and effort and, on the other hand, the ensuring of intelligibility. What we have here once again, then, is the tension which was noted at the beginning of this section, and which was also discussed by Horn (1985) and Levinson (1987, 1988).

The Economy principle has a contributory Maxim of Reduction on the syntactic level, which can be paraphrased as "reduce where possible" (Leech 1983: 67), and which is especially relevant to our purposes, as it deals with pronominalization. As Leech notes:

> The pragmatic point about reduction is that it abbreviates the text, and often simplifies its structure, while maintaining the recoverability of the message. It is when, for some reason, the message's recoverability is impaired that reduction comes into conflict with the Clarity Principle. (Leech 1983: 68)

Our analysis in the following chapters will try to show, first of all, that this conflict indeed exists; secondly, we will propose some criteria for resolving it.

The fourth textual principle, the Expressivity Principle, is less relevant to our purposes. It is concerned with "effectiveness in a broad sense which includes expressive and aesthetic aspects of communication, rather than simply with efficiency" (Leech 1983: 68). It appears to be more relevant to planned or literary discourse than to spontaneous conversation.

2.1.5. An alternative proposal: Economy and Clarity

It is clear that, in discourse, the resolution of the tension between the two pragmatic principles (however they are labelled) is not always straightforward. In fact, the speaker often has to walk the narrow line between, on the one hand, being over-informative, and thus creating unwarranted implicatures by flouting Horn's R-principle, and on the other hand, being too economical, thereby flouting the Q-principle.

A major domain in which this tension can create problems is in the field of pronominalization. Whenever a speaker wants to refer to an entity, he has a variety of choices: he can use a fully lexical NP, he can use a pronominal NP, or he can use a zero-anaphor. Since the latter possibility is to a large extent determined by syntactic factors, we will concentrate on the choice to be made between lexical NP and pronoun. In a lot of cases, the choice will in fact be straightforward; in (13), for instance, the speaker can safely opt for a pronoun:

(13)   *John came in;* he *sat down.*

In (14), on the other hand, he is forced to opt for a lexical NP, as using a pronoun is bound to cause ambiguity:

(14)   *John and Bill came in;* John *sat down.*

Following a line of reasoning similar to Leech (1983), we will suggest the existence of two principles which may be in conflict, and which have a direct impact on the realization of referential expressions, more particularly NPs.

It appears that what the speaker has to do is to make a correct evaluation of the discourse context, and determine to what extent the hearer is able to find an antecedent for the pronominal form he has used; in other words, whether the pronoun is an anaphor. Underlying that decision are the following two principles, which we suggest as alternatives for all the principles reviewed in previous sections:

(15)   The Clarity (C-) principle
            "say as much as you must to avoid ambiguity"
            i.e. use a full NP whenever you have to.

>   The Economy (E-) principle
>   "say as little as you can get away with (given C)"
>   i.e. use a PRO-form whenever you can.

While we agree with Leech (1983) that, in principle, a distinction has to be made between the interpersonal level and the textual level, we think the same principles can be invoked here to deal with both aspects of discourse. For instance, as far as Clarity is concerned, there is no need to distinguish between a textual Clarity principle and an interpersonal Manner maxim ("be clear"), since the construction of a clear *message*   (in Leech's sense; cf. the previous section) presupposes the construction of a clear *text*.   Of course, the latter might not be a sufficient condition for the former, but in the domain of discourse anaphora the "textual rhetoric" is what is primarily relevant.

The following examples show that violating these principles indeed results in inefficient communication. In instance (16), the speaker, by using a pronoun, violates the C-principle, resulting in ambiguity. Instances (17) and (18) below show that violating the E-principle can be similarly disastrous: whereas opting for Economy results in the perfectly felicitous utterance (17), going for maximal Clarity results in the awkward utterance (18), where repetition of the full NP almost forces one into a non-coreferential reading for the two mentions of *John.*

(16)   *John$_1$ and Bill$_2$ came to dinner. He$_{1/2}$ had to leave early.*
(17)   *John$_1$ came in and he$_1$/Ø$_1$ sat down.*
(18)   *?John$_1$ came in and John$_1$ sat down.*

It does appear to be the case, then, that it is important for the speaker to keep a balance between the two principles, making an accurate evaluation of the discourse context.

There are instances where the choice between Economy and Clarity is not so clear-cut, the speaker opting first for Economy by picking a pronoun, then realizing this may endanger Clarity, and thus repairing the pronoun by means of a full NP. This results in a type of repair, not of a real "error", but of a communicative inefficiency, the kind of repair which Levelt (1983) labels "appropriateness repairs". As we will argue in the rest of this chapter, such repair instances show that it is the tension between the two pragmatic principles which results in reprocessing and thus in a repair sequence.

2.2. Types of conversational repair

Since the empirical analysis presented in this study centres around occurrences of conversational repair, it is necessary to be more explicit about what we mean by this notion. Different types of repair can be distinguished, according to different parameters. First of all, we can make a distinction according to which participant initiates the repair, and which participant actually carries it out (cf. 2.2.1). Secondly, we can classify repairs according to what type of "error" is being repaired (cf. 2.2.2). Thirdly, we can classify repairs according to the point in time at which the repair occurs (cf. 2.2.3).

2.2.1. Interactional types of repair

In their influential paper on the repair mechanism in conversation, Schegloff—Jefferson—Sacks (1977) draw a distinction between several interactional types of repair. First of all, a distinction is drawn between the initiation of repair after a trouble-spot (henceforth "initiation"), and the potential outcome of the repair, viz. correction of the trouble-spot (henceforth "correction"). It is important to realize, although this is less relevant here to our purposes, that not all repair-initiations need necessarily lead to correction of the item in need of repair (which we will label the "reparandum", following Levelt (1983), while the repair-item itself will be referred to as the "reparans"). Here, however, we will only be concerned with initiations which also lead to an actual repair.

As far as repair-initiation is concerned, Schegloff—Jefferson—Sacks (1977) make a distinction between initiation by the speaker himself ("self-initiation"), or initiation by another participant ("other-initiation"). Likewise, for correction, a distinction can be made between correction by the speaker who has uttered the reparandum ("self-correction"), and correction by another party ("other-correction"). Combining these different modes of initiation and correction, we thus get four different interactional possibilities:

(19)   self-initiated, self-correcting (=self-initiated self-repair);
self-initiated, other-correcting (=self-initiated other-repair);
other-initiated, self-correcting (=other-initiated self-repair);
other-initiated, other-correcting (=other-initiated other-
repair).

Let us consider some instances of each repair-type, to see what these distinctions mean in practice. The most common repair type, as we will see later on, is self-initiated self-repair:

(20)   *She was givin' me all the people that were gone this year
I mean this quarter.* (from Schegloff—Jefferson—Sacks
1977: 364)

The reparandum *this year* in this instance is self-corrected by the speaker by means of the reparans *this quarter;* furthermore, it is the speaker himself who initiates the repair (cf. *I mean*). In this particular instance, we are dealing with the repair of a lexical error, but obviously repair is not restricted to "errors"; we will return to this in the next section.

By way of contrast, consider a repair which is similar to (20), with the sole exception that it is not the speaker himself, but another participant (which we will refer to as the hearer, for convenience' sake):

(21)   *A: She was givin' me all the people that were gone this year.
B: What? This year?
A: This quarter I mean.*

Signalling that an inappropriateness has occurred is done here by the hearer; nevertheless, it is the speaker who carries out the second part of the repair. We are thus dealing here with other-initiated self-repair.

There are also cases where both initiation and correction are carried out by the hearer:

(22)   *A: She was givin' me all the people that were gone this year.
B: This year? This quarter you mean.
A: Yeah right.*

In this instance of other-initiated other-repair, the hearer both signals a trouble-spot and provides the reparans (which is then acknowledged by the speaker in the next turn).

The fourth and last type of repair is self-initiated other-repair, although this is actually quite rare:

(23)   A: *She was givin me all the people that were gone this year*
               I mean...
        B: *This quarter you mean.*
        A: *yeah right.*

In this instance, the speaker signals the existence of a trouble-spot, but it is the hearer who carries out the actual correction. As we will see later on, this type of repair is very infrequent, for straightforward reasons.

Schegloff—Jefferson—Sacks (1977) rightly point out that these types are not simply alternative possibilities, but that conversation is so organized that self-repair is more likely to occur than other-repair:

> Rather, the organization of repair in conversation provides centrally for self-correction, which can be arrived at by the alternative routes of self-initiation and other-initiation —routes which are themselves so organized as to favor self-initiated self-repair. (Schegloff—Jefferson—Sacks 1977: 377)

This observation naturally follows if one considers the places in the flow of speech where repair can be initiated, viz. in the reparandum-turn (opportunity 1), in the transition space following this turn (opportunity 2), or in the other-turn following the Transition Relevance Place (or TRP) (opportunity 3). Levinson (1983: 341) summarizes the preference ranking as follows:

(24)   Preference 1 is for self-initiated self-repair in opportunity 1
               (own turn);
        Preference 2 is for self-initiated self-repair in opportunity 2
               (transition space);
        Preference 3 is for other-initiation in opportunity 3 (next turn),
               of self-repair (in the turn after that);
        Preference 4 is for other-initiated other-repair in opportunity 3
               (next turn).

It will be observed that both opportunity 1 and 2 favour self-initiated self-repair, and that opportunity 3 may still lead to self-repair. It can also be predicted from this that self-initiated other-repair is virtually impossible. In what follows, we will show that the collaborative process of referent-tracking can lead to all the types of repair discussed here, but also that the types are open to refinement.

The most favoured form of repair is thus the self-initiated, self-correcting one; most RDs in fact fall into this category. Other studies (e.g. Moerman 1977 for a Thai corpus) show that this preference for self-initiated self-repair is not restricted to English conversation, but may be universal.

Since self-initiated self-repair is most frequent, and since this is the repair type we will deal with most of the time in this study, it is worthwhile to go a bit deeper into this. Self-initiated repair can occur in either of three positions in the turn-taking sequence:

(25)   (a) in the same turn as the trouble-spot source;
        (b) in the TRP (transition relevance place) of that turn;
        (c) in the turn subsequent to the one following the trouble-
            source turn, the so-called "third turn".

We will encounter all three possibilities in our data. For more details on repair, we refer the reader to the discussion in Levinson (1983: 339ff.).

The repair mechanism has important repercussions on conversational syntax, as it can reorganize utterances drastically; Schegloff (1979) observes: "(...) in some respects, the operation of repair in sentences is like a super-syntax. It can order and reorder the arrangement of the components of the sentence as well as restructure its overall shape" (Schegloff 1979: 280). We will return to this in due course.

2.2.2. Error-repair versus appropriateness-repair

In the preceding section, we have classified repairs according to their interactional characteristics. We can also, however, make distinctions on the basis of what kind of trouble-spot it is which is being repaired. Levelt (1989) distinguishes between error-repair (or E-repair) and appropriateness-repair (or A-repair). As the name suggests, E-repair is concerned with the correction of errors; these can be lexical, phonological, morphological, or syntactic in nature. The examples in the previous section, for instance, are all instances of (lexical) E-repairs. In this study, we will *not* be concerned with E-repairs, since the phenomena we are dealing with cannot be considered to be "errors" in the strict sense of the word.

The other type of repairs Levelt labels A-repairs. These repairs replace an item which is less felicitous in the speeech situation in which it occurs by a more appropiate one. An example:

(26)   *I'll come over the day after tomorrow; Tuesday I mean.*

The repairs that are discussed in this study bear a close resemblance to A-repairs, in that they have more to do with felicitousnness than with errors; we will argue, however, that they constitute a repair type in their own right, which we will label Informativeness repairs (or I-repairs for short).

Levelt (1983) only deals with self-repairs; he distinguishes three different stages in the repair process:

(27)   interruption of the flow of speech;
        use of editing terms;
        making of the repair.

We will return to the interruption of the flow of speech in the following section.

Initiation of the repair can, but need not, be marked by the use of editing terms. Editing terms are not especially frequent with A- or I-repairs; the most common ones in our data are *I mean* and *that is*.

As far as the making of the repair is concerned, Levelt (1983, 1989) shows convincingly that, as far as their format is concerned, repairs observe certain constructional restrictions; he formulates the following well-formedness rule for repairs, (A stands for the original utterance, G for the repair):

(28)   A repair <A G> is well-formed if and only if there is a string B
        such that the string < AB and* G> is well-formed, where B is
        a completion of the constituent directly dominating the last element
        of A. (*and to be deleted if G's first element is itself a sentence
        connective).

This rule correctly predicts the well-formedness of (29), as shown by the application in (30); it also correctly predicts the ill-formedness of (31):

(29)   *[To the right is a green,]$_A$ [a blue node]$_G$*
(30)   *[To the right is a green]$_A$ [node]$_B$ and [a blue node]$_G$*
(31)   *[Did you go right,]$_A$ [you go left]$_G$*

The well-formedness rule, however, does not always appear to apply to the repairs discussed in this study, as we will see later on (in chapter 10).

2.2.3. Temporal aspects of repair

Depending on the point at which the flow of speech is interrupted, we can make, first of all, a distinction between what we will label immediate repairs and delayed repairs, respectively. In immediate repairs, as the label suggests, the repair is carried out right after the reparandum constituent; e.g.:

(32)   *He, John I mean, came to visit me yesterday.*

In delayed repairs, on the other hand, the repair is carried out at the end of the utterance containing the reparandum; e.g.:

(33)   *He came to visit me yesterday, John I mean.*

Delayed anaphor repairs often lead to a format which can be labelled "RD" (see chapter 6); immediate repairs will be discussed in chapter 8.

This corresponds to a distinction made by Van Wijk (1987) between retracing and non-retracing repairs. In retracing repairs, "the speaker interrupts her ongoing speech more or less abruptly, backtracks to an earlier point of the utterance and repeats it in a fully or partly modified form" (Van Wijk 1987: 38). In non-retracing repairs, on the other hand, "the reparandum is replaced without any backtracking" (Van Wijk 1987: 38).

Finally, a distinction can also be made between repairs which do not repeat any part of the original utterance (apart, of course, from the item which is being replaced), such as (33), and repairs which do so, as in (34) below:

(34)   *He* came to visit me, *John* came to visit me yesterday.

The latter type of repairs will be discussed in chapter 8.

2.2.4. Repair of inadequate reference forms

In this study, we will be dealing with the way speakers repair a pronominal form which has unclear reference by means of a more informational lexical noun phrase. In particular, we will show that instances of other-initiated self-repair and self-initiated self-repair provide evidence for the tension between the pragmatic principles discussed in section 2.1. In a lot of these cases, the outcome of this repair process falls under the syntactic heading of "RD".

Not all cases of pronoun-to-noun repair, however, are realized as RDs. We can also get other-repairs (chapter 7), or repairs which for other reasons fail to meet the criteria for qualifying as a RD (chapter 8). The repair mechanism for inadequate reference forms can also lead to the repairing of a noun by a more informational noun (cf. chapter 9).

We will show that the four interactional types of repair (cf. 1.2.1) indeed show up in the data, but that Schegloff—Jefferson—Sacks' (1977) classification is in need of refinement in certain respect. First of all, we will argue that it is not always possible to draw a sharp distinction between self- and other-initiation of repair; for instance, some self-repairs have in fact an element of other-initiation in them. The same is true to some extent for self- and other-correction. Secondly, we will argue that the notion of "repair" itself may be somewhat too limited, in that there are phenomena which are not, strictly speaking, repairs in the true sense, but are nevertheless repair-related (e.g. the question-RDs in chapter 6).

On the whole, our data confirm Schegloff—Jefferson—Sacks' (1977) claims about the preference for self- over other-initiation, and for self- over other-correction. It should be pointed out, however, that self-initiated, other-correcting repair is by far the least common repair type, for reasons which will be discussed in due course.

We could also argue that the repairs discussed here are a special type of A-repairs (Levelt 1983); indeed, inadequate reference forms cannot be regarded as E-repairs, in that no real "error" is made, but rather a violation of the principle of Clarity discussed elsewhere. We believe, on the basis of that C-principle, however, that there is sufficient reason to regard referential repairs as a repair form in their own right, since a lot more is involved than the mere replacement of an "inappropriate" form, reference-establishment being such a crucial matter. We will thus claim there to be a category of "Informativeness-repairs" (or I-repairs) to which the repairs discussed in this study belong.

2.3. Information flow in conversation

2.3.1. Preliminaries

In this section, we will be mainly concerned with those aspects of discourse which have received a lot of attention in the discourse-analytic literature, and which have usually been discussed under headings such as "givenness" or "thematicity" (see also Geluykens 1992). Terminological confusion and, worse, theoretical vagueness abound in the literature. With this in mind, we have proposed an alternative concept for the analysis of information flow in conversational discourse in general, and for the analysis of anaphor repair in particular. This notion we will label *Recoverability*.

Although this section refers to a lot of DA work, and although the notions we will be using are to some extent related to DA notions such as Givenness, it must be emphasized straightaway that our work differs from most DA work in several important respects. First of all, as has already been pointed out (chapter 1; Geluykens 1992), DA work suffers from a profusion of a priori theoretical apparatus. This apparatus is then, afterwards, applied to the data, exceptions being considered "quantitatively insignificant". We will be working the other way round: we will let the data dictate which theoretical concepts are needed for an analysis which is sufficiently explanatory. For the sake of expository clearness, this theoretical section necessarily precedes our data-analysis; this, however, is not an accurate reflection of our methodology. It should thus be kept in mind that the concepts introduced here are in fact "data-generated";

their usefulness stands or falls with the confrontation with the data. If it can be shown that they can be usefully applied to the database, this will justify their existence. This methodology has in fact more in common with the CA tradition than with DA work.

Secondly, care is taken that our notions do not suffer from the same shortcomings as most DA notions, viz. vagueness and unfalsifiability. This criticism is summed up by Prince (1981), who states in her discussion of the given-new taxonomy:

> this (...) notion has never received a satisfactory characterization that would enable a working linguist (...) to actually put it to use. (Prince 1981: 225)

In our analysis, the most important criterion for our characterization of recoverability is that it should be operational, i.e. directly applicable to conversational data, without any danger of subjective interpretation. Our definition will depend directly on the discourse context, rather than on notions such as the hearer's consciousness (Chafe 1987).

Thirdly, and finally, we differ from most DA work in the importance we attach to the interactional aspect of discourse. Whereas most DA authors tend to view discourse solely as information transmission, we think that it is impossible to analyze conversation properly without taking its interactional dimension into account. In fact, these two aspects cannot be separated, in the sense that an information flow account of some phenomenon can never on its own constitute a sufficient analysis; RD is a clear example of this, as will be shown in chapters 3 to 5 below. Conversation is, by its very nature, always interactional; the information flow account is thus in a way subsidiary to the interactional one, as we will attempt to show in our discussion of repair.

We will briefly review here the discussion of givenness offered by Prince (1979, 1981). She argues that givenness can be defined in terms of three possible parameters: Predictability, Saliency (or Consciousness), and Shared Knowledge. Most authors have indeed defined Givenness in one of these three terms. To give but a few examples: Halliday (1967, 1985; Predictability), Chafe (1976, 1987; Saliency), H. Clark (Haviland—Clark 1974, Clark—Haviland 1977, Clark—Marshall 1981; Shared Knowledge) (for a review of the literature, cf. Geluykens 1984). Rather than going into all these definitions separately, we will consider Prince's summary (Prince 1981: 226-230) in some detail, as also done in Geluykens (1992):

(35)   Givenness$_p$ (Predictability): The speaker assumes that the hearer
            can predict or could have predicted that a particular linguistic item
            will or would occur in a particular position within a sentence
        Givenness$_s$ (Saliency): The speaker assumes that the hearer has
            or could appropriately have some particular thing/entity/... in
            his/her consciousness at the time of hearing the utterance
        Givenness$_k$ (Shared Knowledge): The speaker assumes that the
            hearer 'knows', assumes or can infer a particular thing (but is not
            necessarily thinking about it).

Before going into the usefulness of these definitions, two things can be observed right away. First of all, note that all of them are in terms of speaker-assumptions; this makes them inherently unverifiable, as there is no way we can have direct access to the assumptions the speaker makes. It may well be that the givenness status of a linguistic item depends, ultimately, on speaker-assumptions; however, it might be wiser to disregard this and to develop concepts which are, first and foremost, operational. We will try to show that speaker-assumptions can in fact be left out of the picture. Secondly, these definitions abound with expressions such as "could have predicted", "could appropriately have", and the like, which makes them very hard to verify empirically.

Ignoring these problems for the time being, it can be observed that the three characterizations given above are not mutually independent. If a speaker assumes that an item is predictable, he can assume that it is in the hearer's consciousness; if he can assume it to be in the hearer's consciousness, the latter probably has some knowledge about it. These dependencies, however, do not run the other way: not everything the hearer "knows" can be assumed to be in his consciousness, and not everything which is in his consciousness need be predictable. We will have a look at each of the three types of givenness, and discuss why they are inadequate for our purposes.

2.3.2. Givenness and Shared Knowledge

Let us start with the broadest definition, viz. Givenness$_k$ (Shared Knowledge). Shared Knowledge is a very broad term indeed, as it incorporates not only the knowledge shared by the participants by virtue of the previous discourse record (both verbal and non-verbal), but also all the "background knowledge", i.e. knowledge about the organization of the world, etc. This array of knowledge is so vast (cf. Clark—Marshall 1981) as to render it virtually useless for deciding which elements are given and which are not. It is clear that not all Shared Knowledge can be treated as given: since discourse participants tend to have a vast store of knowledge which is shared, this would simply make almost any piece of information given.

The term Shared Knowledge is also misleading, since it fails to distinguish between general background knowledge (cf. Dik's (1978: 128) "general information") and knowledge arising from the discourse context ("contextual information", ibid.). Haviland—Clark (1974: 512), for instance, define given information as "what the listener is expected to know already", but fail to specify what exactly they mean by "know".

Naturally, long-term knowledge of the world is important in language processing, but in a less direct manner. Consider the following example, which is an actual instance from our data:

(36)   *I've got this job in a teacher training college. They're not university calibre obviously, the students (cf. S.1.6.16.4).*

The referent *they (the students)* is not new here, even though it is not actually present in the preceding context. This is because the fact that "colleges have students" can be considered part of the "college" Scenario (cf. Sanford—Garrod 1981) or Frame (Goffman 1974, Fillmore 1975) (see Brown—Yule 1983: 238-256 for a review). As we will see in this study, this does influence linguistic structure (i.c. in a lot of the repairs discussed later on; cf. chapter 5), but it does so by virtue of contextual factors, because the referent *the students* is inferable from the context, not because it is Shared Knowledge. Givenness$_k$ is thus not sufficiently useful as an analytical tool.

2.3.3. Givenness and the Hearer's Consciousness

Let us now turn our attention to Givenness$_S$ (Saliency or Consciousness); according to this line of reasoning, given information is defined as that information which the speaker assumes to be in the hearer's consciousness. The psychological claim which this definition makes is its main attraction, but at the same time its major weakness; there is no way of empirically validating whether an element is given or not, as we have no access to what is in the hearer's consciousness and what is not. What is more, the speaker does not have this either; he can only make reasonable assumptions based on the context (admittedly, in Chafe 1976, this is pointed out).

By context we mean the complete discourse record of a discourse at any given point, including both linguistic and situational information. From the analyst's viewpoint, only close scrutiny of this context can give us a clue as to the givenness status of an element. In analyzing the context, we have an advantage over the speaker, by virtue of the interactional nature of conversational discourse; this is pointed out by Levinson (1983):

> Conversation, as opposed to monologue, offers the analyst an invaluable analytical resource: as each turn is responded to by a second, we find displayed in that second an analysis of the first by its recipient. Such an analysis is thus provided by participants not only for each other but for the analyst too. (Levinson 1983: 321)

The context is thus the main factor which will be taken into account in determining givenness; we will return to this in section 2.3.5.

In a recent paper, building on earlier work (Chafe 1976), and dealing with "cognitive constraints on information flow" (Chafe 1987), Chafe proposes a new treatment of the problem how to describe adequately the information flow in discourse. In that paper, too, the given-new distinction is treated in terms of what the speaker considers to be (or not to be) "in the focus of the hearer's consciousness". Chafe proposes a threefold division into *active* (what the speaker assumes to be in the hearer's consciousness), *semi-active* (what the speaker assumes to be in the hearer's peripheral consciousness), and *inactive* (what the speaker does not assume to be in the hearer's consciousness) information. These activation states are a direct reflection of cognitive activity.

While we agree with Chafe's insight that information flow in discourse can be characterized partly in terms of varying activation states, we want to claim here that there is an additional interactional dimension which plays a vital role in information flow, and that the cognitive dimension as defined by Chafe must be complemented by, and is ultimately even dependent on, the interactional one which we will highlight here. The emphasis which Chafe puts on the purely cognitive and informational side of discourse originates from a pre-occupation with precisely that type of discourse which is least interactive, viz. narrative. Thus, when Chafe claims to say something about "spontaneous spoken language" (Chafe 1987: 21), he is really drawing conclusions from an excerpt of spontaneous spoken narrative, which does not exhibit the normal turn-taking characteristics present in the most frequent and least restricted type of spoken discourse, viz. conversation. In real conversation, where the interactional dimension is far more outspoken, the dependence of cognitive processing (as defined by Chafe) on interaction can be shown more clearly, as we hope to show below.

This dependence should be understood on two discrete levels. First of all, on a micro-level, in conversational discourse, there are interactional constraints governing the flow of information. The way information is organized, and its treatment as either given or new information, depends crucially on speaker-hearer collaboration, as realized through the turn-taking system (see also Geluykens 1988b, 1991, 1992, 1993; Geluykens—Goossens 1989); no theory of information processing can afford to neglect this dimension.

A second interactional dimension operates more on the macro-level, and has to do with the fact that conversational discourse is, in essence, goal-oriented. In other words, the transmitting of referential information can, but need not, be the primary goal in a piece of discourse. Information transmission is only one of the possible conversational "activities" which can be performed by the speaker, and this activity may in fact be subsidiary to a more important goal, such as for instance a request sequence. This dimension is less relevant to our current analysis, but its existence must be recognized.

From the outset, Chafe makes it clear that the linguistic phenomena he deals with, in particular the distinction between given and new information, are "manifestations of basic cognitive processes, and that we can never understand them fully until we understand the psychological phenomena underlying them" (Chafe 1987: 21). The whole problem of information flow is discussed in purely cognitive terms. As we have pointed out, Chafe goes on to make a threefold distinction, based on what activation state a concept is in, into active, semi-active, and inactive concepts (Chafe 1987: 25):

(37)   Active concept: one that is currently lit up, a concept in a
          person's focus of consciousness.
          Semi-active concept: one that is in a person's peripheral
          consciousness, a concept of which a person has a background
          awareness, but which is not being directly focused on.
          Inactive concept: one that is currently in a person's long term
          memory, neither focally nor peripherally active.

The purpose (and result) of communication, then, is to effect changes
in the activation states of concepts in the consciousness of the hearer.

The claim that the given-new (or active-inactive) status of concepts
has a cognitive grounding, depends on what is or is not present in the
participants' consciousness, and thus ought to be redefined in
psychological terms, is of course a very sensible one. Information
flow is thus looked upon as a cognitive process dynamically
unfolding through time. What Chafe does not recognize, however, is
that the cognitive activity expressed through discourse is always, in
essence, also an interactional phenomenon. Interaction plays a vital
role in information flow, a fact which is virtually ignored by Chafe.
Our basic claim, which is a crucial amendment to Chafe's claims, is
that the cognitive dimension of information flow must necessarily be
regarded as dependent on the interactional one.

The other main criticism of Chafe's characterization of information
flow is that it is, once again, dependent on speaker-assumptions, and
on assessments about what can be considered to be in the hearer's
consciousness, which makes the concepts of only limited use for the
analysis of actual data. What we need is a more practical, operational
characterization of information flow.

2.3.4. Givenness and Predictability

This leads us to the third type of Givenness, viz. Givenness$_p$
(Predictability). The seminal definition here is the one offered by
Halliday (1967), who defines New information as non-predictable,
"not in the sense that it cannot have been previously mentioned, (...),
but in the sense that the speaker presents it as not being recoverable
from the preceding discourse" (Halliday 1967: 204).

Given information, then, is information which is presented as
being recoverable from the preceding discourse.

The advantage of this definition is that it is in terms of recoverability from the preceding context; we have already argued that the context should indeed be the decisive factor. However, ultimately, the definition is equally unoperational. The problem lies in the qualification "presented by the speaker as ...", since it leads to circularity. The only way of assessing whether the speaker actually presents a predictable item as given is through its linguistic realization. We argue against making such apriori assumptions concerning the linguistic expression of functional notions, as it would make such notions circular. The only way the analyst has of judging givenness is through recoverability, through the actual presence or derivability of an element in the context. Whether this reflects the speaker's assumptions is neither here nor there; hopefully, if he makes invalid assumptions, such as presenting a non-predictable item as given, this will be made clear by subsequent hearer response. The notion of "previous mention" is thus more important than would appear from Halliday's definition.

Moreover, the notion of Predictability used by Prince is confusing, since it suggests that, for an item to be given, it has to be predictable at a specific place in the utterance; in our view, this is not the case. We will therefore employ the term recoverability, which does not have such connotations.

2.3.5. Towards an operational alternative

We have shown all three definitions of givenness to be deficient for some reason, and are now in a position to propose an alternative. Since the terms given-new are so over-used and confusing, it would be better to avoid them altogether, and to replace them by the notion of Recoverability. Information can thus be either *Recoverable* or *Irrecoverable* (see also Geluykens 1992).

(38)   Recoverable information is information which is derivable from the discourse record, i.e. from the context.

(39)   Irrecoverable information is information which is not derivable from the discourse record.

This derivability can be either relatively direct (when the information is explicitly present in the preceding clause, for instance) or more indirect (as in (36) above, where certain inferences have to be made).

It can be deduced from the way we have defined recoverability that it is not to be regarded as a simple binary distinction. Since derivability can be either direct or indirect, there are clearly degrees of recoverability (similar, but not identical views are held by Firbas 1964, 1965, 1966; by Prince 1979, 1981; by Hannay 1985b; and, as we have seen above, by Chafe 1987). What is involved is a recoverability scale (see also Geluykens 1992, 1993):

(40)   100% Recoverable ——————— 100% Irrecoverable.

Underlying this scale is a complex of factors, which we will now discuss in some detail.

The first, and most important, factor we will label *Inferability* (the term is borrowed from Prince (1981), but used in a slightly different sense here). Directly recoverable items do not need a lot of inferencing to deduce their status; an example is *he* in (41):

(41)   *Steve likes beans; he also likes toast.*

(note that even such simple examples actually need an inference to make the connection between *Steve* and *he*). Irrecoverable items cannot be derived from the context, no matter how many inferences are made; an example is *John* in the context of (42):

(42)   *Steve likes beans; John, on the other hand, likes toast.*

In between such extremes are cases like *the students* in (43), which is a slightly simplified version of (36) above:

(43)   *I've got a job in a college; the students aren't very bright.*

The referent *the students* is to some extent recoverable, but not as directly as the *he* in (41); it can be indirectly inferred by virtue of the college-scenario. We will call such elements inferables; an inferable is thus an element which is situated somewhere between the two extremes of the recoverability scale in (40). In Chapter 5, we will show inferability to be relevant for the analysis of the informational status of RD (and also for other repairs).

There are two other factors, which are not on the same level as inferability, but which also have an influence on the Recoverability status of an item: *Interference* and *Distance* (the terms themselves are borrowed from Givón (1983), but distance is used in a less quantitative manner here).

When an item has not been mentioned for some time, its recoverability clearly devaluates. We will refer to this intervening factor as distance, but will not consider distance to be a strictly linear, quantitative measure, depending simply on the amount of intervening material between two mentions of a referent; clearly, it is the nature of the intervening material which is important here as well as the amount. We will return to this in Chapter 5. Interference is exemplified by (44):

(44)   *John likes Bill; he loves Mary.*

Let us assume that *he* is supposed to be coreferential with *Bill*; it would then normally be fairly directly recoverable. However, the element *John* can be said to "interfere" with the recoverability status of *he*, since it is an equally plausible candidate for coreference (*John* having the same number and gender as *Bill*). Note that interference is on a different level than inferability and distance, as it is not really concerned with a referent's cognitive status; also, it is only relevant when one is dealing with pronominal (and thus potentially ambiguous) elements.

2.4. The Database

2.4.1. Organization of the corpus

Our functional analysis in the following chapters will concentrate on conversational discourse. The database contains 350,000 words of conversation, i.e. seventy files taken from the Survey of English Usage. There are three main subdivisions in this database:

(45)   surreptitiously recorded face-to-face conversation
                 (36 files; 180,000 words);
            non-surreptitiously recorded face-to-face conversation
                 (24 files; 120,000 words);
            telephone conversation (surreptitiously recorded)
                 (10 files; 50,000 words).

These are all the conversational Survey files currently available. The
rest of this section gives some more information on the files
employed in this study.
First listed are the surreptitious face-to-face files. Note that some
participants in these files are not recorded surreptitiously ("NS" =
non-surreptitious); these, however, are not included in the word
count for the files; nor are they included in the analysis (there are a
few cases, however, which are included):

S.1.1 (2 participants, both male; intimates);
S.1.2 (2 participants, both male; intimates);
S.1.3 (3 participants (2 NS), 1 male, 2 female; intimates);
S.1.4 (2 participants, both male; intimates);
S.1.5 (4 participants, all female; intimates);
S.1.6 (2 participants, 1 male, 1 female; intimates/equals).
S.1.7 (3 participants (1 NS), all male; intimates);
S.1.8 (3 participants, all female; intimates);
S.1.9 (4 participants (1 NS), 3 male, 1 female; intimates/equals);
S.1.10 (3 participants (2 NS), 1 male, 2 female; intimates/equals);
S.1.11 (3 participants (1 NS), 1 male, 2 female; intimates/equals);
S.1.12 (4 participants (2 NS), 2 male, 2 female; equals);
S.1.13 (3 participants (1 NS), 2 male, 1 female; equals);
S.1.14 (3 participants (2 NS), 2 male, 1 female; intimates/equals);
S.2.1 (2 participants, both male; intimates);
S.2.2 (2 participants, all male; equals);
S.2.3 (3 participants (1 NS), 2 male, 1 female; equals);
S.2.4 (4 participants (2 NS), 3 male, 1 female; intimates/equals);
S.2.5 (3 participants (1 NS), 2 male, 1 female; intimates/equals);
S.2.6 (4 participants (1 NS), all male; intimates/equals);
S.2.7 (3 participants (1 NS), 1 male, 2 female; intimates/equals);
S.2.8 (4 participants (2 and 1 NS), 1 male, 3 female; intimates);
S.2.9 (3 participants (2 NS), 2 male, 1 female; equals);
S.2.10 (4 participants (2 NS), 2 male, 2 female; equals);

S.2.11 (2 and 4 participants (1 & 2 NS), 2 male, 2 female; int/eq);
S.2.12 (2 participants (1 NS), both female; intimates/equals);
S.2.13 (4 participants (2 NS), 2 male, 2 female; intimates/equals);
S.2.14 (3 participants (1 NS), 1 male, 2 female; intimates/equals);
S.3.1 (3 participants (1 NS), 2 male, 1 female; disparates);
S.3.2 (2 participants, 1 male, 1 female; disparates);
S.3.3 (6 participants, 4 male, 2 female; disparates);
S.3.4 (6 participants, all male; disparates);
S.3.5 (3 participants (1 NS), all male; disparates);
S.3.6 (7 participants (1 NS), 6 male, 1 female; disparates);

The second list consists of non-surreptitious face-to-face conversations:

S.4.1 (2 participants, 1 male, 1 female; intimates);
S.4.2 (2 participants, 1 male,1 female; intimates);
S.4.3 (2 participants, 2 male, 2 female; equals);
S.4.4 (4 participants, 3 male, 1 female; equals);
S.4.5 (3 participants, 1 male, 2 female; intimates);
S.4.6 (4&5 participants, 2 male, 2&3 female; equals);
S.4.7 (3 participants, 1 male, 2 female; intimates);
S.5.1 (5 participants, unknown gender; equals);
S.5.2 (5 participants, unknown gender; equals);
S.5.3 (3 participants, unknown gender; equals);
S.5.4 (5 participants, unknown gender; equals);
S.5.5 (5 participants, unknown gender; equals);
S.5.6 (4 participants, unknown gender; equals);
S.5.7 (4 participants, unknown gender; equals);
S.5.8 (2 participants, 1 male, 1 female; equals);
S.5.9 (2 participants, 1 male, 1 female; equals);
S.5.10 (2 participants, both male; equals);
S.5.11 (2 participants, both male; equals);
S.5.12 (6 participants, gender unknown; equals/intimates);
S.6.1 (2 participants, gender unknown; disparates);
S.6.2 (2 participants, 1 male, 1 female; disparates);
S.6.3 (2 participants, gender unknown; disparates);
S.6.4 (3&2 participants, 2 male, 1 female (2 female); disparates);
S.6.5 (4 participants, gender unknown; disparates);
S.6.6 (2 participants, gender unknown; disparates);
S.6.7 (2 participants, gender unknown; disparates);

The final list consists of telephone conversations:

S.7.1 (intimates);
S.7.2 (intimates);
S.7.3 (intimates);
S.8.1 (equals);
S.8.2 (equals);
S.8.3 (equals);
S.8.4 (equals);
S.9.1 (disparates);
S.9.2 (disparates);
S.9.4 (disparates);

These files consist mostly of short conversations with both male and female participants; in our telephone conversations, there are only two participants.

As far as the relationships between the participants is concerned, we get the following:

intimates: 16 files (80,000 words);
equals: 24 files (120,000 words);
intimates/equals: 14 files (70,000 words);
disparates:16 files (80,000 words).

A bit over 44% of this database (31 files out of 70) consists of dialogues; the remainder varies from 3 up to 7 participants, from both sexes. The result is a fairly representative database of conversational discourse (there are of course some problems with the representativeness of the Survey as a database; cf. for instance Owen's (1982) review of Svartvik—Quirk [1980]).

2.4.2. The system of prosodic analysis

The prosodic system used in this study is the one developed by Crystal (Crystal 1969, 1972, 1975; Crystal—Quirk 1964). Crystal belongs to the so-called "British school" of prosodic analysis (cf. Ladd 1980 for a review); other exponents of this tradition are Kingdon (1958), O'Connor—Arnold (1961), Halliday (1968, 1970), Bolinger (1958, 1986), Brazil (1975, 1978), Brown—

Currie—Kenworthy (1980), and Cruttenden (1986). We have chosen to work with Crystal's system (as in Geluykens 1992), not merely because of its practical convenience (it is the system used in the Survey files), but also because it is, arguably, the most comprehensive theory currently available for the English language.

In the remainder of this section, we will briefly sketch Crystal's theory (cf. Geluykens 1986a: 21ff. for a more extensive discussion). The basic premiss is that there are a number of psycho-acoustic parameters in speech (such as pitch, speed, loudness, silence, and rhythm), from which we can derive a number of perceptively salient prosodic features.

One of these features is Intonation, which is associated mainly with pitch range and pitch movement (in the British school, one works with "configurations" rather than with "levels" of speech, cf. the discussion in Bolinger 1958). Another feature is sentence accent, for which we take over Halliday's distinction between Tonality (the division of speech into prosodic units, or "tone units") and Tonicity (the location of sentence accents —or "nuclei"— within these tone units). Other features are Tempo (associated with speed), Rhythmicality (rhythm), and Pauses (this temporal aspect of speech is very relevant to our analysis, as will be seen in later chapters). Three prosodic features will receive our special attention: pauses, tonality-tonicity, and intonation. Other features will not be taken into account, except in passing.

The basic unit of prosodic analysis is the tone unit (or TU for short). It consists of a Nucleus (the syllable —or syllables— carrying the main pitch movement), optionally preceded by a Head (ranging from the first pitch-prominent syllable —the Onset— up to but not including the Nucleus), which in its turn can be preceded by a Pre-head (everything preceding the Onset); the Nucleus may be followed by a Tail (which in most cases carries on the pitch movement of the Nucleus). The basic structure of a TU is thus:

(46)   (pre-head) onset (head) nucleus (tail)

The only obligatory part of the TU is thus the Nucleus (which is also the Onset if there is no Head present).

As for intonation, three types of nucleus are possible: simple, complex, and compound. Simple tones include Falls, Rises, or Level tones. Complex tones are either Fall-Rises or Rise-Falls. The most common compound tones are combinations of a Fall and a Rise (Fall + Rise, or Rise + Fall); compound tones thus have two nuclei instead of of one. When we talk about a "rising tone" in our analysis, we mean a tone ending in a rising pitch movement; this can be a rise, a fall-rise, or a fall + rise. Similarly, a "falling tone" can be a fall, a rise-fall, or a rise + fall.

2.4.3. Transcription Conventions

The following prosodic symbols are used in the database.

intonation: simple tones: fall: `x; rise: ´x; level: -x
               complex tones: fall-rise: `´x; rise-fall: ^x
               compound tones: rise+fall: ´x `x; fall+rise: `x ´x

other: tone unit boundary: #
               onset: /
               non-nuclear stress: ' (normal); " (heavy)
               subordinate TU: [...]   (= also phonetic transcription)

pauses: very brief: .
               brief: -
               longer: --
               long: ---

Note that pauses in the Survey are transcribed related to speech rhythm, "-" representing a pause of approximately one foot long.

In addition to the prosodic symbols mentioned above, the following are used:

speaker identity: A; B; C; ... (surreptitious)
                     a; b; c; ... (non-surreptitious)
overlapping speech: *...*; **...**
intranscribable or dubious: ((...)); ((sylls))
glottal stop: [?]; dental fricative: [th]; palatal fricative: [sh]; schwa [∂]
Survey reference numbers: e.g. S.1.2.3.4 = file 1.2, slip 3, line 4
reparandum + reparans: underscoring

Chapter 3

Other-initiated self-repair

3.1. Introduction

The first type of data we will tackle in our empirical analysis are those in which hearer-initiation of the repair is followed by speaker-correction. Although this is not the most frequent type of repair (which is only to be expected if one considers the preference pattern generated by the repair opportunity places, which heavily favours self-initiated self-repair), we think it makes sense to start our discussion with this type, as it is the one in which initiation of the repair is signalled explicitly by the hearer. Other-initiated self-repair thus permits us to establish a non-controversial pattern for the interpretation of anaphor repairs; we can then expand this pattern, in later chapters, to other interactional types of repair.

In the next section, we will look at the prototypical interactional process involved in the repairing of problematic anaphors; we will show that these repairs follow a typical three-stage pattern. In section 3.3, we will discuss repairs which are self-correcting, but in which this self-repair occurs after an attempt at other-correction; this category of repair is interesting, as it is a kind of mixture of self- and other-correction. In section 3.4, finally, we will discuss some variants on the interactional three-stage process.

3.2. The prototypical repair process

To start off this section, and to start off our empirical analysis of anaphor repairs, let us consider an instance of other-initiated self-repair in detail:

(47)   *B: so there # -- now oh dear what "/`else do I 'have to*
               ´say to them # to /cheer <u>them</u> `up # --
          *A: cheer who up *-* --*

> *B: *(- sighs)* ((the)) / `family # --- Nan went off today - .*
> *(S.4.2.77.2)*

This repair is typical of the repair data we will encounter over and over again in this and the following chapters. In this exchange, speaker B first produces an utterance with a pronominal element (viz. *them*), thereby going for maximal Economy by pronominalizing a referent which he judges to be sufficiently anaphoric (we will go into the reasons for this in chapter 5). Speaker A then indicates, in the next turn, that B's opting for Economy has resulted in problematic processibility of the pronoun, and that the speaker has thus violated the Clarity principle by being insufficiently non-ambiguous; in other words, speaker A initiates an informativeness repair. Speaker B reacts to this initiation by offering a fully lexical alternative NP (viz. *the family*) which is coreferential with his original pronoun, thereby restoring Clarity. Such exchanges are good evidence of the tension which exists between Economy on the one hand, and Clarity on the other hand, as there is a clash between what the speaker opts for (viz. the minimal linguistic expression available) and what the effect on the hearer is from the point of view of referential interpretation (viz. failure at disambiguation). Such clashes, as we will see, occur over and over again.

Let us first resolve some terminological matters. From here onwards, as mentioned earlier, we will often refer to the item-to-be-repaired (i.e. the original pronoun) as the "reparandum", and to the item replacing the pronoun (i.e. the full NP) as the "reparans", to indicate their respective functional status. As an alternative semantic terminology, we will refer (for reasons which will become clear in chapters 4 and 6) to the utterance containing the reparandum as the "proposition" (or PROP for short), to the reparans-NP as the "referent" (or REF), and to the reparandum-pronoun as the "gap".

In the following sections, we will classify other-initiated repairs according to the type of initiator being used by the hearer to trigger the repair.

3.2.1. Explicit marking of the trouble spot

First of all, we can distinguish repairs in which the hearer marks the trouble spot to which the initiation refers in an unambiguous way, by specifically marking that he has a referential problem with the reparandum. Instance (47) above is in fact such an initiation, since by using the expression *cheer who up,* the hearer marks that the problem lies in the identification of the object-pronoun of *cheer up* in the PROP.

There are other examples of this kind of repair-initiation in the data, which is only to be expected, as this is an effective way of repair-initiation. Below are some more examples:

(48)   *A: well are these chaps left high and dry now without*
            a job*
          *B: *oh no* . no no they're they're covered . in fact . [ə]*
            because . [ə] Prendergast goes on to [ə:m] a
            Yiddish literature . expansion post in two years
            time # - and /Harrington has ((the)) money .
            earmarked from the existing <u>one</u> `´anyway # [ə]
            to the /end of three `years # at the /end of ´that
            *time # he /goes over`seas # *((I / ´take it #))**
          *A: *[ə] [ə] [ig]* from the existing what*
          B: thi thi thi /`first # - the /[fə] <u>the /first twenty thousand</u>
            <u>`pounds</u> # (...) (S.1.2.47.13)

(49)   [this is a NS instance; hence the absence of prosodics]
          c: now I've now I've lost <u>it</u> .
          B: what have you lost my dear
          c: much to my shame - <u>my Bluff your Way in Music</u> ---
          B: oh well I'll bring a copy of mine next time
            (S.2.10.68.1)

(50)   *B: why do you think that deserves to be . put in a*
            category called problem plays -
          A: because of [thi:] . ((the)) so many untied strings there
            are in the play and [thi] sort of . [ə:m] (- coughs) -
            the difficulty of interpreting [ə:m] - (((thi:])) [thi:]
            the views and [thi:] [ə:m] . the themes expressed
            in the play
          B: do you mean that you . it's called a problem play
            because we don't know what it means - really
            we haven't settled the question ((really))

> A: *well there's /no general a`greement <u>on it</u> I should*
>   *`think #*
> B: *on what .*
> A: */on [∂:m] -- /on '[thi:] [∂:m] - the /mixed up `bits in*
>   <u>*the play*</u> *# [thi:] [∂:m] (S.3.5.a32.7)*

The prototypical repair process exemplified by (47) to (50) above can be summarized in the following manner:

(51)   stage 1 (speaker A): utterance with pronominal reparandum
       stage 2 (speaker B): initiation of repair
       stage 3 (speaker A): repair though fully lexical reparans-NP

We will see that this three-stage process is indeed the prototypical, interactionally favoured way of correcting a problematic anaphor, and that the interactional variations occurring in the data underlyingly also have the pattern in (51) at their basis.

The following is a slight elaboration of the three-stage process outlined above, in that the trouble spot is not resolved straight away:

(52)   B: *((and)) he said well I'm sorry ((you know)) we*
               don't cater for this you'll just have to change
               your timetable or work at home ((so)) I said this
               just means I shall do half as much work # ((and))
               he /said `very well # .
           A: */[k] `who `said `this #*
           B: *the / `secretary # *.* of the / `school #*
           A: **/I `m #** /who's `that #*
           B: */George `For nby # (S.2.4.a37.3)*

What appears to happen here is the same as happens in the preceding examples, with one crucial difference. Speaker B first utters, following the Economy principle, the pronominal form *he* in the first turn. This gives rise to other-initiation of the repair by speaker A in the second turn. Speaker B then repairs the pronoun by means of the lexical NP *the secretary of the school*. After this, speaker A is still not able to establish successful reference, and thus again has to prompt speaker B to provide more precise information (in other words, the Clarity principle was still not sufficiently adhered to).

Speaker B then duly provides a more informational NP, i.c. *George Fornby*. We can summarize this as follows:

(53)   stage 1 (B): utterance with reparandum (pronoun)
            stage 2 (A): repair-initiation
            stage 3 (B): first attempt at reparans (full NP)
            stage 4 (A): prompt for more information
            stage 5 (B): second attempt at reparans (full NP)

It is clear that this schema can be reduced to the prototypical interactional process in (51) above.

3.2.2. Trouble spot marking through *wh*-word

The hearer can also mark the trouble-spot in a less direct manner, and initiate a repair simply by indicating that he has some (unspecified) problem with the speaker's original utterance. This is the case, for instance, in (54) below:

(54)   [this is a NS instance, hence the lack of prosodics]
            b: what sort of jobs do they get after .
            A: what .
            b: your students - *(S.1.10.153.8)*

In this exchange, speaker b produces a PROP with the reparandum *they* (first turn). Speaker A then indicates that he has a problem with the PROP, by producing the repair marker *what* (second turn); this repair-initiation could in theory be concerned with any aspect of the preceding utterance. Speaker b, however, interprets it (correctly, as it turns out), as referring to the fact that the hearer has a problem with establishing the right reference of *they,* and replaces it by means of the reparans *your students* (third turn). We thus get the same three-stage reference-resolving process.

Let us consider another instantiation of this type of repair-initiation in some detail:

(55)   *A: charming chap you know he's got absolutely* -- .
            none [ari] . no religious taboos at all you know .
            it is he's really fitted in awfully well --

> B: yes /*that* would be rather un((`common)) -
> A: *what*
> B: *to /have no [?ð:m] . sort of . food ta`boos ((and 'so forth*))
> A: *yes he hasn't he drinks and he'll eat anything (...)*
>   *(S.1.6.61.1)*

What appears to happen here is the following. Speaker B utters a proposition with a pronominal gap (i.e. *that*), after which a TRP (short for Transition Relevance Place, cf. chapter 2) is reached. As we have seen before, this is a place where repair may be initiated, and this is precisely what happens: speaker A expresses his uncertainty about the proposition by uttering the "question" *what,* and thus signals that a repair is in order. The repair-initiator is then interpreted —rightly, as it turns out— as expressing the hearer's uncertainty as to the precise reference of *that.* In the third turn, therefore, B self-corrects his original utterance by providing a semantically more specified referent (which in this case happens to be an entire state-of-affairs, expressed by a non-finite sub-clause, rather than a single referential expression), viz. *to have no...food taboos.* In fact, in more "traditional" terms, the REF might in fact simply be labelled an (elliptical) answer to the *wh*-question *what.* Be that as it may, the fact remains that we are dealing with a repair mechanism here. What we have, then, is a three-stage interactional process along the lines summarized in (51) above.

There are other instances of this type of repair in our data,. Instance (56) below is in fact almost identical to (54-55):

(56)   B: *no no that's a funny . expression # that's "/really `weird #*
        d: **what**
        B: **the* ex/pression Cau'casian **meaning white `skinned #***
        d: ***Caucasian for race .** mhm . (S.2.11.b75.4)*

Once again, the repair-initiation *what* is rightly interpreted as a problem of inadequate reference, and the initial gap *that* is replaced by a full lexical referent (again clausal in nature). Some more examples:

(57)   A: (...) - /was he /wasn't <u>he</u> re'fused the `chair in
                    'Oxford #
            ns: who
            A: / '<u>Skeat</u> # wasn't he re*'fused*
            ns: *that's Meak*
            A: /oh `Meak # yes (...) (S.1.9.145.3)

(58)   a: and everybody will know it's snide and no-one
                    will take it seriously .
            B: /she 'says 'no thank you 'very 'much but '<u>she</u>'s too
                    ` 'busy # or /something 'dedicated # --
            a: who's that
            B: /<u>Doctor `Annabel</u> # . (S.2.5.a2.8)

Note that in (57), there is another referential problem, caused by the
fact that the first speaker turns out to have the wrong person in mind.

3.2.3. Trouble spot marking through discourse signal

There is one instance in the data in which repair is initiated in yet
another way, viz. through the use of a discourse marker:

(59)   A: . [∂] there was the most [?∂] [ma:] rather marvellous
                    shadow play # /which would [∂:] /you /[thi:] rest
                    of the `Senate # /were in "'fact [in the /`end #] #
                    con/spiring to `kill <u>him</u> you 'see *.*
            B: */'mhm #*
            A: [<u>Ca/'ligula</u> #] #
            B: B: yeah (S.7.1.c6.10)

In this exchange, repair is initiated by the hearer's uttering of the
short discourse signal *mhm,* uttered with a rising intonation contour.

3.3. Self-repair after attempt at other-repair

In this section, we will look at some repairs which are other-initiated,
but in which the hearer also makes an attempt at other-correction.
This attempt, however, turns out to be unsuccessful, and thus
eventually leads to self-correction by the original speaker. Such

repairs are, as it were, halfway in between the other-initiated self-repairs discussed above and the other-initiated other-repairs discussed in chapter 7.

An example of this is (60) below, in which the repair-initiation is more specific than in the previous instances, since speaker c already provides some candidates for co-reference with the Gap *she* in B's PROP:

(60)   B: *and be/sides <u>she</u> always 'comes `down [in the*
            / `summer #] #
          c: *your sister *. or your mother**
          B: **[ə] <u>my /sister and</u>* my `mother # . / `both of them #*
            (S.1.12.122.6)

In this instance, the context leaves two likely candidates for the reference of *she*. The hearer explicitly shows that the speaker has not been explicit enough, and that reference is still unclear; this inadequacy is duly resolved by the referent *my sister and my mother* (it thus turns out that both referents were meant). In other words, the process in (51) is once again involved here.

There are two other instances of this type of self-repair after attempt at other-repair in the data, viz. (61) and (62) below:

(61)   A: *I like that one best - the ((tree)) in the middle - but*
            I /think it's too [ə:] <u>it</u> would "/ `dominate the
            'room [a /bit too `much #] #
          C: */what the `´checkerboard # .*
          A/ *[ə] /no <u>the `´next one</u> # - (S.1.8.40.2)*

(62)   A: *I mean . the thing is I know what I have to do is*
            work an awful lot at night I mean . you know
            *I've taken that into account # - *. I'm /going to*
            have to do a `lot of <u>it</u> #*
          a: **[ə:] you mean domestic work at night**
          A: *"/ `no # . ((a /lot of)) "`<u>reading at 'night</u> #*
          a: *yes (S.3.1.a7.6)*

Instances such as these show that there are in fact more than four possible interactional types of repair; we will return to this later on.

3.4. Some interactional variants

In this section, some repair processes will be discussed which are inter-actionally slightly different from the ones discussed in previous sections, in that they involve a process which is a bit more complex than the one outlined in (51) above.

First of all, consider instance (63), which is interactionally similar to the instances already discussed, but is realized in a somewhat different manner:

(63)   A: (...) --- *hasn't some Canadian recently set up a*
            a foundation you're not in fact Canadian though
            are you
        B: *no .*
        A: *no -*
        B: *no that's my trouble # /that was my `trouble # with*
            ap/plying for a Canada `Council # /you `see #
            ((and it)) -
        A: *what*
        B: *I /say that was my `trouble # in [plain in tr] in*
            ap/plying for a Canada `Council # - "/not being
            *a Canadian *-**
        A: **yeah**
        B: *`citizen # you / `see #*
        A: *hm - (S.2.1.64.4)*

This instance is similar to the previous ones, in that the repair is other-initiated. The speaker, however, rather than merely providing a fuller lexical specification for the pronominal *that* in his first mention of *that was my trouble...* (turn 4 in the transcript), chooses to repeat his original utterance almost literally, and only then provides the full lexical referent. The result is a structure in which no hearer-turn intervenes between PROP and REF; at the basis of this, however, lies the same three-stage strategy, the only difference being its actual realization, which can be represented as follows:

(64)   Stage 1:   Proposition (1st mention) (speaker 1)
        Stage 2:   repair-initiation (speaker 2)
        Stage 3:   Proposition (2nd mention) + Referent
                   (=repair) (speaker 1)

This already shows what will also be shown in another section, viz. that the actual realization of the repair is to some extent accidental; it is the underlying mechanism which is more interesting from a functional point of view.

An important point has to be made about the structure resulting from stage 3 in exchange (63) above. It should be noted that what we get there is the concatenation of a complete clause (the second mention of the PROP) and a "bare" constituent (the REF), i.e. a constituent (which happens to be a sub-clause in this instance) which is not the argument of any following verb. What we have, then, is a PROP + REF structure which has the syntactic characteristics of the construction which is usually labelled "right-dislocation" (after Ross 1967; henceforth "RD") in the literature. In the next chapter, where we will discuss self-initiated self-repairs, we will come across similar structures. In chapter 6, we will go into the consequences of this link between the syntactic construction RD and the discourse process of repair.

As a final example, and as a preliminary to the following chapter, let us consider an instance which is a mixture of self- and other-initiation, both processes occurring virtually simultaneously :

(65)   B: (...) --- *those two are quite all right but they are*
                        unsuitable for [thi: ∂m] occasion aren't they -
             A: **yes**
             B: *they're *sort of* pieces*
             A: *yes -*
             B: *you want a big room . **for those***
             A: ***mhm** # . /yes <u>this</u> is the 'one I could most*
                        `'live `with # . *((<u>the cardinals</u>))*
             B: **((<u>the statues</u>))**
             A: */well <u>the `cardinal</u> 'actually #*
             B: *yes - the cardinal is a sort of . costume piece*
                        (S.1.8.18.8)

In this exchange, speaker A utters a proposition with the pronominal gap *this,* after which a pause occurs (we will discuss the interactional relevance of such pauses in great detail in the following chapter). He then realizes that his reference might be inadequate, and thus repairs it by means of the referent *the cardinals.* Simultaneously, however, the hearer has also realized he cannot precisely identify the reference of this, and thus makes an educated (but mistaken) guess, viz. *the statues*. This (other-)initiation overlaps with the speaker's initial self-repair, so that he is more or less forced to repeat his reparans (albeit in the singular rather than the plural this time). Instance (65) might be schematically represented in the following way:

(66)   —Stage 1 (speaker 1): PROP + REF (1st mention)
                (=self-repair)
            —Stage 2 (speaker 2): Initiation of repair
                [overlaps with REF]
            —Stage 3 (speaker 1): REF (2nd mention) (2nd repair)

This process is thus an interesting mixture of the other-initiated process described above, and the self-initiated ones discussed in the next chapter. As such, it provides indirect evidence for our analysis of RD in terms of collaborative repair (cf. chapters 4 and 6). It also shows that there is more to repair, interactionally speaking, than a simple distinction between self- and other-initiation and self- and other-correction.

    As far as the prosodic aspects of other-initiated self-repair are concerned, these will be discussed, along with the prosody of self-initiated self-repair, in chapter 4.

3.5. Conclusion

In this chapter, we have attempted to show empirically that the Economy amd Clarity principles indeed operate in conversational discourse, and that there is an inherent tension between them which can lead to a clash, which in its turn can lead to the initiation of a repair. This chapter has dealt with other-initiated self-repairs; in the following chapter, we will deal with self-initiated self-repairs.

    All these repairs, apart from providing empirical evidence for the validity of our pragmatic principles, also show that the tracking of referents in conversation is a collaborative process depending crucially on speaker-hearer co-operation (see also Geluykens 1989b). This collaborative dimension, which will show up constantly in our data, is an important factor in the process of reference-tracking (and that of referent-introduction); cf. Clark—Wilkes-Gibbs (1986);

Geluykens (1988b); Geluykens (1993), which depends very much on hearer-feedback.

We have already touched upon self-initiated self-repair to some extent in the previous section (3.4). We have pointed out that some of these repairs result in what could be labelled, from a structural point of view, a "RD". This is even more the case for the repairs discussed in the next chapter. Later on, in chapter 6, we will discuss the syntactic implications of this in more detail.

Chapter 4

Self-initiated self-repair

4.1. Introduction

In this chapter, we will attempt to show that instances of self-initiated self-repair also provide evidence for the pragmatic tension between the Clarity and Economy principles. By providing empirical evidence for the claim that referent-tracking depends on speaker-hearer feedback, we will also show that reference is a collaborative process.

The other claim made in this chapter, and one of the principal claims of this study, is that RD is not really a "construction" as such, but an, as it were, accidental realization of this interactional process, whereby an utterance is repaired by adding on a NP (the REF) which is semantically more informational than an element in the original clause (the gap). In most cases (i.e. all repairs discussed in this chapter) this repair is self-initiated (although we will argue there to be an element of other-initiation; in fact we will argue that there is no sharp boundary between self- and other-initiation of repair, the difference being more a matter of degree), but in some instances, it is other-initiated (cf. the previous chapter). We will return to the syntactic and functional status of RD in chapter 6; in this chapter, we will be concerned with the interactional dimension of self-initiated self-repair.

4.2. Interactional analysis of self-initiated self-repair.

4.2.1. Self-repairs with intervening pause

In this section, we will discuss repairs in which there is no intervening turn between PROP and REF. Unlike the ones in the previous section, both initiation of the repair as well as correction of the reparandum are done by the speaker himself. Although we label these "self-initiated", we will claim that there is an element of (implicit) other-inititation as well.

We will start by looking at some typical cases of self-repair (with a simple NP as the REF). The most important feature of these is the occurrence of a *pause* between PROP and REF; we will argue this pause to be an important interactional feature in its own right. A good example is (67) below; this comes from a context in which speakers A and C are looking through a collection of paintings (these are thus part of the extralinguistic context):

(67)   A: *well I don't think I want to ((2 sylls)) you know they're*
              a bit too sort of strong .
        C: **mhm**
        A: **for* my room - so I thought I'd wait till he he had*
              another lot
        C: ***mhm***
        A: ***I** /like \`that 'one best # - the /((tree)) in the \`middle*
              # - but I think it's too [ə:] it would dominate the room
              a bit too much
        C: *what the checkerboard .*
        A: *[ə] no the next one -*
        C: *yes (...)   (S.1.8.40.1)*

We argue the pause to signal the repair-initiation, in the same way as the intervening hearer-turn initiating the repair in the cases discussed in chapter 3. The pause can thus be regarded as an interactional stage in its own right, the interactional structure being the following:

(68)   Stage 1: PROP (speaker 1)
        Stage 2: initiation of Repair (pause)
        Stage 3: REF (speaker 1) (=repair)

In detail, what happens in (67) is the following. The speaker utters a PROP with a pronominal element (i.e. *that one*), which he thus judges to be recoverable (see chapter 5) by the hearer from the context. However, he then judges the precise reference of this Gap to be problematic for some reason (in this case, as there are quite a number of likely candidates for coreference with the Gap in the non-linguistic context, viz. all the paintings present in the room, there is likely to be confusion). Contrary to the instances in chapter 3, where this reference problem was signalled explicitly by the hearer, the speaker himself initiates the repair without any explicit verbal prompting. The pause, however, can be considered to signal the speaker's self-initiation of the repair; we will return to this shortly. After the pause, the speaker "corrects" the Gap by substituting a more informative lexical NP, the outcome being, once again, a RD. Note that, despite this repair, the problem in (67) is still not completely solved: there is still some ambiguity as to the precise reference, as can be deduced from the subsequent context, in which the hearer still asks for more information.

Before we go more deeply into the significance of the pause in interactional terms, let us have a look at some similar examples:

(69)   B: (...) - you know _she_ /was old and 'on her ^own . # _my_
          /auntie 'Elsie *and* # . if she had
       c: *mhm*
       B: something like knitting (...) (S.1.12.113.2)

(70)   A: because when you've got these two things which are .
          [∂] . essentially alien . being bound up with one another
          one's future - . and . how one learns at university # -
          /that . /that . an`noyed me # - _the ir/`relevance # of /these_
          'two [`things] to each `other # -- (S.5.9.35.1)

(71)   A: (...) [∂:m] . you /know [?] you /don't know 'how _it's_
          `'got there # . _the par/ticular con`dition_ # . often -
          you can see it's there . and is harmful yes . (...)
          (S.2.9.103.6)

(72)   B: ((but)) there is such a thing as # [ø] and /_this_ was
          "^almost 'news to me # . _/risk . `management_ # /that is
          # you . say -- (...) (S.2.11.b112.4)

(73)   A: (...) it was tatty and it was quite dirty # but _it_ /was ex-
          `'pensive # -- */`'you know the # _the /`tables_* # and
       a: *mhm - yeah* (S.2.12.72.8)

(74)   C: well that's all watercolour I think both those books
       b: yeah --

C: [ə:m] . ((2 sylls)) - I /think it looks as 'though <u>it</u> 'works
    very `well # - <u>their /method of . 'repro`duction</u> # -
    (S.4.4.36.3)

(75)   B: (...) certainly when I send chapters in and # /they
        <u>they</u> /come [`back] with a blue `pencil # - <u>a /lot of</u>
        <u>the `good bits</u> #
        A: ((yeah)) -   (S.3.6.49.2)

In all these instances, there is a pause between PROP and REF, a
pause which is "silent" i.e. linguistically realized as absence of any
overt signal. Note also the overt repair marker *that is* in instance
(72), which confirms our analysis of these cases in terms of repair.
We will go into the prosodic evidence in favour of a repair analysis in
section 4.3.

In other cases, for instance in (76) below, the pause is voiced
rather than silent:

(76)   A: (...) - I /do ⌃know <u>those</u> # [ə] <u>the [th th:] [ə] /beautiful</u>
        ⌃<u>blooms</u> # or /`blossoms # /`'there # but [ə:m] my
        memory being poor what are they . (S.4.4.87.8)

Other hesitation phenomena occur as well, as in (77):

(77)   B: [ə:] if not Imola Cyprus - which is once again I think
        having a bit of an up and up - [ə:m] under Craig
        de Leon I may be *wrong*
        A: *yes* . yes . I [kwai] I quite agree there
        B: I think this is a possibility *.*
        A: *yes*
        B: [ə:m] - or [ə:m] - just possibly Rimini # ((<u>it</u>'s a /bit small
        `scale # I /think [?] `Rimini # and it may not be that we
        can be very much help to it yet ((2 or 3 sylls))
        (S.1.2.38.13)

In this particularly case, there is a glottal stop between PROP and
REF, which is also a typical hesitiation marker.

Let us now consider the significance of pauses in a bit more detail,
and explain why they form evidence for our analysis in terms of
repair. Note, first of all, that pauses occur after an outspoken TRP,

viz. the PROP, which is a syntactically and semantically complete unit in its own right. Having said this, we will offer two interpretations of pauses in self-repairs, which are in fact complementary sides of the same phenomenon.

The first interpretation might be labelled cognitive, in that it views the occurrence of a pause in terms of processing. Indeed, the pause can be seen as a signal of the reprocessing which is done by the speaker, the reprocessing needed to repair an unfelicitous part of the utterance. Since we are dealing with unplanned discourse, the speaker has to produce and evaluate utterances as he goes along; this is why repair is so frequent in unplanned, conversational discourse. In our repairs, the speaker first utters an utterance with a pronominal gap (the PROP); he then realizes, however, that he has not been informational enough, i.e. he has realized the Gap to be inadequate for the hearer to establish accurate reference to the intended person or object. This realization comes, naturally, after the uttering of the Gap —otherwise the speaker would have used a full lexical NP in the first place— and probably, on the evidence of the pauses, comes after the entire PROP has been uttered. The pause, then, reflects the speaker's evaluation that something is inadequate, and the time it takes him to re-process the PROP and add a reparans-NP to it.

When we translate this cognitive interpretation into more interactional terms, the pause thus reflects the self-initiation of the repair mechanism by the speaker. The speaker himself recognizes some conversational inadequacy, which takes him a short time, and enhances the adequacy of his utterance by self-correcting it by means of a self-initiated repair. The cognitive explanation thus also has an interactional dimension to it.

However, there is a second, even more interactional interpretation, which does not contradict the first, but which makes the repair not merely a matter of self-initiation, in that it implicitly includes the hearer into the picture. Indeed, since conversation always involves more than one participant, this aspect should always be taken into account.

In terms of speaker-hearer interaction, then, the following can be said. First of all, we have already pointed out that the position just behind the PROP is an obvious TRP, since the PROP is a syntactically (and prosodically, cf. elsewhere) complete unit. This does not mean that the hearer should be expected to take over the floor at all times, but it does mean that an opportunity is given for

56   Chapter 4

him to do so. The TRP character of the position after the PROP is very much strengthened by the fact that the speaker pauses at this point: as soon as one participant stops talking, this is obviously an ideal opportunity for someone else to take the floor, especially if the silence occurs at a point which is already, for structural reasons, a TRP. In other words: the end of the PROP, in combination with the pause, puts quite a lot of pressure on the hearer to take the floor.

Yet, as we see in our examples, in the majority of cases the hearer does *not* take the floor. In our interpretation, this serves as an implicit element of other-initiation of the repair mechanism for the speaker. Put differently: the fact that the hearer does not continue at a point where he might be expected to do so, serves as an additional cue for the speaker that something is wrong, and that a repair of some kind may thus be in order. We are thus suggesting that, although repairs with a pause are to a large extent self-initiated, in that there is no verbal contribution from the hearer to set the repair going, there could nevertheless be an element of other-initiation involved. This other-initiation consists of the fact that the hearer does give some (tacit) non-verbal signal, viz. he does not take over the floor at a point where there is every chance for him to do so. In fact, the possibility should not be ruled out that the hearer contributes even more actively in the initiation of the repair, viz. by giving some non-verbal cues (gestures, eye movement, frowning, etc.); of course, the nature of our database makes it impossible for us to check on this.

To sum up: in interactional terms, pauses between the PROP and the REF can mean the following. First of all, they can be interpreted as reflecting the speaker's self-initiation of a repair sequence: the speaker realizes he has made insufficiently explicit reference, then pauses as it were for thought, and corrects the inadequate reference by means of a REF. Secondly, from the hearer's point of view, the pause reflects a TRP which is not being used, which can be read by the hearer as a cue that a repair is due; this is the other-initiated element. Note that these two interpretations are perfectly compatible, as soon as one accepts that repair need not necessarily be either 100% self- or 100% other-initiated, but that the initiation of some repairs can be the result of an interactional process between the speaker and the hearer. Our findings thus force us to view the repair mechanism as being more subtle than a matter of a process being triggered by either speaker or hearer. This being said, the element of self-initiation in RDs with pauses is more obvious, and less controversial, than the other-initiatited element; hence the title of this chapter.

It should be pointed out that this interpretation of pauses in self-repairs is of course to some extent speculative, in that there is no direct way of checking the precise impact of the pause in interactional terms. However, apart from the arguments already given, there is corroborating evidence for our analysis, in that there is a correlation between the ocurrence of pauses and the conversational function of RD. Indeed, as we will see in chapter 6, RDs which do not function as repairs (and which will be discussed in some detail) tend *not* to have pauses between PROP and REF; this suggests that the pause is of some interactional value in repair-initiation.

4.2.2. Self-repairs without intervening pause

There are a number of structures which appear to function as repair mechanisms, but in which there is no pause between PROP and REF. It has to be concluded, then, that the occurrence of a pause is by no means a necessary condition for a RD-type structure to be regarded as being a repair (nor is it a sufficient one: there are RDs with a pause which are not repairs, as we will see in chapter 6).

In fact, there are only a few instances of RDs with a NP-REF which are pauseless and which nevertheless function as repairs. Instances (78-80) are some of the clear cases:

(78)   *B: is term all *right**
       *A: *yes* it seems all right so far . touch wood (- laughs)*
       [ǝm] I've still got [t] the one other girl arrived today
       # they're still /"coming in in dribs and ᴧdrabs #
       the /`new ones # (S.7.1.c16.6)

(79)   *a: what about [thi:] kind of situation that begins with Lear .*
       where you get him dividing up his kingdom . isn't that
       *equally a kind of donné . *for the tragedy**
       *A: *yes* it is # and [i] it's /often been - `criticized #*
       ((the /`way)) # that it's /just
       *B: **by whom -- by whom***
       *A: **. im`mediately . [/slipped `in #] # -** (S.3.5.b44.3)*

(80)   *A: I got this lecturing job in a teacher's training college -*
        B: mhm .
        A: which is quite fun # I [`mean] 'they're `not # /uni`versity
            `calibre # /`obviously # the /students 'on the `whole #
            (...)   (S.1.6.16.4)

There are other pauseless RD-like structures, which also function as repairs, but in which the REF is not a NP; these will be discussed in chapter 6.

   We should point out that these pauseless repairs do not constitute real counter-evidence for the repair-analysis offered in the previous sections. Although a pause between PROP and REF is a strong repair-initiation indicator, it is not the case that initiation of repair depends in a crucial way on the presence of a pause. Whether followed by a pause or not, the position just after the PROP remains an obvious TRP, and the fact that speaker-change does not occur may thus still be significant. Moreover, the fact that there is no pause may merely mean that in these repairs the element of other-initiation discussed earlier is completely absent; in other words, these are purely self-initated repairs, in contrast to the ones in chapter 3 (other-initiated) and in the preceding section (mainly self-initiated).

4.3. Prosodic aspects of Repair-RDs

4.3.1. Preliminaries

In this section, we will attempt to show that the prosodic behaviour of self-repairs indirectly confirms our interactional account of them as a collaborative referential repair strategy. Three aspects of prosody will be investigated. First of all, we will pay some attention to the temporal behaviour of self-repairs, i.e. especially to the occurrence of pauses, voiced pauses, hesitation phenomena, turns, etc. between PROP and REF, insofar as we have not yet done so in previous sections. Secondly, we will have a look at the tonality (tone group boundaries) and tonicity (placement of the nucleus) of self-repairs. Thirdly, and perhaps most importantly, we will investigate the intonation of self-repairs, especially the final pitch movement of the PROP, which is interactionally the most significant tone, as it is the pre-TRP pitch movement. The prosody of other-initiated self-repairs will be discussed at the same time. (Note that only repairs with an NP as their reparans are taken into account here; clausal REFs (cf. chapter 6) are not included.)

4.4.2. Pausal behaviour of self-repairs

Table 1 recapitulates the respective frequencies of the different types of repair discussed in this and the preceding chapter. These figures show that almost 60% of our data have either a turn or a pause (or both) between PROP and REF. Since we have argued this turn or pause to be interactionally and cognitively relevant —they represent respectively other-initiation of the repair and other-prompted self-initiation of the repair— their high frequency does not come as a big surprise. Note also that, although a pause can be an important signal for the initiation of a repair, it is by no means a necessary condition; the end of the PROP (whether or not followed by a pause) is a TRP in its own right, and the speaker may elect to start a repair without pausing (in which case it is self-prompted rather than other-prompted).

Table 1. Occurrence of pauses/turns in self-repairs

	absolute frequency	relative frequency
[+ Turn]	15 (+2 NS)	(16%)
[+ Pause]	44	(46%)
[- Pause]	37	(38%)
Total	96	(100%)

Finally, as a point in favour of our interactive interpretation of pauses in self-repairs, we should point out that there is a significant difference in the frequency of occurrence of pauses in repair-RDs as opposed to non-repair-RDs (the latter will be discussed in chapter 6, where we will also return to their prosody in greater detail). Table 2 indeed shows a significant difference between the two major functional categories (repair and non-repair). This difference also indirectly confirms our functional classification in terms of repair and non-repair.

Table 2. Occurrence of pauses/turns in repair- vs. non-repair-RDs

	repair-RDs	non-repair-RDs
[+Pause/Turn]	59	6
[-Pause/Turn]	37	23

4.3.3. Tonality and Tonicity of self-repairs

Turning our attention now to the occurrence of a tone unit boundary between PROP and REF, we will again make a distinction between repair-RDs and non-repair-RDs. It should be clear that we have already, in an indirect way, discussed tonality, for, whenever there is a pause or a turn in between PROP and REF, in most cases this implies that there is also a tone unit boundary between the two parts of the RD. Table 3 deals only with the [-pause] cases.

Table 3. Occurrence of tone unit boundaries in repair vs. non-repair RDs

	repair-RDs	non-repair-RDs
# PROP # REF #	37	6
# PROP REF #	—	17
Total	37	23

Two things can be deduced from this table. First of all, the figures show that the REF of repair-RDs virtually always has a separate tone unit from the PROP or, put differently, that the REF always has a separate tonic nucleus (or nuclei) in its own right. Secondly, table 3 shows a significant difference between repair-RDs and non-repair-RDs in this respect.

The fact that the REF in self-repairs carries one or more nuclear tones fits in quite well with what one would expect. In self-repairs, due to the fact that the REF is used as the reparans for a pronominal form, it is important that this reparans gets some prosodic prominence, to facilitate comprehension for the hearer, and thus to ensure the resolving of the referential problem.

As far as the reparandum is concerned, this almost never receives any form of prosodic highlighting. This confirms that the speaker regards it as unproblematic at first, and only later realizes it to be in need of repair.

4.3.4. The intonation of repair-RDs

The most important prosodic feature, in interactional terms, of self-repairs is surely the final pitch movement of the PROP, as it precisely there that the repair is being initiated. Table 4 shows the final tones on the PROP, and divides them into falling and rising tones. These figures clearly show the high frequency of falling tones on the PROP, and once again offer strong, independent evidence in favour of the interactional account offered in previous sections. Indeed, the PROP of self-repairs is much more likely to end in a falling tone (75%) than in a rising tone (25%); out of the falling tones, a simple fall is by far the most frequent tone.

Table 4. Final tone on PROP in self-repairs

Fall	09	28	24	61	(64%)
Rise-Fall	—	04	05	09	(9%)
Rise	02	—	02	04	(4%)
Fall-Rise	01	08	01	10	(10%)
Fall + Rise	03	04	04	11	(11%)
No tone	—	—	01	01	(1%)
FALLING	09	32	30	71	(74%)
RISING	06	12	07	25	(26%)
Total	15	44	37	96	(100%)

We claim that this intonational behaviour strongly supports our claim that these structures are indeed to be regarded as instances of referential repair. Although determining the function of falling versus rising tones in the turn-taking system is not a straightforward problem, recent research by others (see Cutler—Pearson 1986) and by ourselves (see Geluykens 1986a, 1988c) does suggest one thing, viz. that a rising tone seems to be used by speakers to signal non-finality of a turn, i.e. the fact that the speakers wants to hold the floor and continue his turn. A falling tone, on the other hand, is more likely to signal turn-completion, i.e. the fact that the speakers offers other participants an opportunity to take the floor. Also, rising intonation is often used to signal non-finality of an utterance; it occurs, for instance, often between a subordinate clause and a main clause.

Table 5 shows the distribution of rising tones in general in conversation according to their discourse location (taken from Geluykens 1988c, which is a study based on an extensive corpus of conversational data).

Table 5. Discourse locations of rising tones

	absolute frequency	relative frequency
neither clause- nor turn-final	701	59.7%
clause-final but non-turn-final	1630	25.7%
clause- and turn-final	399	14.6%

Distinguishing between the different types of rising tone (rises, fall-rises, fall+rises), the following tendencies were observed:

(81)   Rises (simple rises) are often used to signal the non-finality of an utterance; hence they are often found on a non-final phrase, or on the first part of a complex sentence. They are also often used to signal non-finality of a turn, to signal that the speaker wants to carry on.
Fall-rises are likewise often used to signal the non-finality of either an utterance (very frequently) or of a turn (less frequently).
Fall+rises are also often used to signal non-finality of an utterance (less frequently) or of a turn (very frequently).
(Geluykens 1986a: 41)

Rising intonation thus often signals non-finality of utterance and/or turn. This incompleteness or non-finality marking function is also claimed by other authors (see Bolinger 1982, 1986; Cruttenden 1981, 1986).

Given this assumption, the high frequency of falling tones in self-repairs can be interpreted as follows. First of all, from a cognitive point of view, they signal that the speaker, at the time of utterance, probably regards the utterance as complete, not only from a syntactic point of view (which of course it is, strictly speaking), but also from the point of view of regarding it as being communicatively appropriate and sufficiently informative (i.e. as observing the C-principle). It is only after uttering the complete PROP that he realizes it to be not as informative as it should be, by virtue of the unclear reference of the Gap. In other words, this argues for a *procedural* account of repair, where the speaker plans the utterance as he goes along (which accounts for the fact that repair appears to be restricted to unplanned discourse; after all, in planned discourse, any repairing work can be done in advance), and *re*-organizes it after realizing its communicative inefficiency. This realization appears to come at a point in time when at least part of the PROP has already been uttered; hence the falling tone. The intonation of self-repairs thus argues against regarding RDs as being merely syntactic constructions, in the sense of them being one of the various ways in which the order of constituents can be realized. On the contrary, RD is a *process*, relying on collaboration, whereby an utterance which was previously regarded as felicitious is re-shaped drastically (see also chapter 6).

One can also look at the occurrence of falling tones from a more interactional angle. It must be noted from the outset that this angle is not incompatible with the cognitive account we have just offered. On the contrary, the cognitive account forms part of the interactional account in a way, in that it is precisely the highly interactional nature of conversational discourse which forces the speaker into the kind of reprocessing described above.

From an interactional point of view, then, one can say that the falling tone on the PROP marks it, even more outspokenly, as a TRP, i.e. as a place where the floor can be taken over by the hearer. Note that it is a TRP anyway, by virtue of its syntactic completeness (and by the frequent occurrence of a pause after the PROP). Despite this outspoken TRP, the hearer does *not* take the floor, which we claim to reflect the fact that he does not regard the utterance as entirely appropriate (naturally, there may be other reasons why the hearer does not take the floor, but the turn-internal occurrence of a falling tone does remain a striking fact). This inappropriateness might lie in the fact that the utterance is not informative enough from a referential point of view, due to the occurrence of a semantic gap. In some cases, this is enough to trigger hearer-repair-initiation (cf. the repairs in chapter 3), but in most cases, this does not occur. In quite a number of cases, though, the fact that the hearer does not take the floor even after a pause is significant. Although we do not claim that this pause is actually a repair-initiation signal on the part of the hearer, we do want to claim that he contributes to the repair, albeit in a passive way, and that it is thus not totally self-initiated. We have called such a process "other-prompted" self-initiated repair; this term reflects the fact that in these cases, there is no strict boundary between self- and other-initiation.

Interestingly, table 4 shows a slight correlation —albeit not a very significant one (all significance levels are calculated using X^2 tests; the significance level is set at .001)— between the use of a falling tone and the occurrence of a pause (or turn) between PROP and REF, in the sense that pauseless repairs tend to have a PROP ending in a falling tone even more often than do other repairs (81% vs. 69%). This in fact also ties in with our account: if there is no pause, the falling tone becomes very important, as it is then the only prosodic turn-finality marker present; on the other hand, if there is a pause, this has some chance of being regarded as a turn-yielding signal, even if the preceding tone is non-falling. However, a combination of pause and falling tone is of course communicatively more effective, as is shown by the high frequency of falling tones even in self-repairs with pauses.

Putting the interactional and cognitive accounts together, one might summarize as follows. The falling tone, often in combination with a pause, indicates first of all, from the speaker's point of view, self-initiation of the repair: the speaker utters a syntactically complete utterance adhering to the E-principle, realizes it might violate the C-principle, and repairs it by means of the REF; in the case of repairs with a pause, this repair is other-prompted, i.e. the hearer passively contributes to the speaker's self-initiation of repair. Secondly, from the hearer's point of view, the falling tone (and the pause), create an outspoken turn-completion signal at the TRP, at which point he can do either of two things. First, the hearer can himself initiate a repair mechanism, which results in other-initiated self-repair (which is relatively rare, cf. chapter 3). Alternatively, the hearer can simply decline to take the floor. The latter has two effects: it creates an opportunity for the speaker to re-organize his utterance (thus creating a self-repair); moreover, it may also function as a signal for the hearer that some pragmatic principle is violated, that there is a trouble-spot. In the first case, the repair is purely self-initiated; in the second case, though repair is still self-initiated, the hearer does contribute, albeit passively, to the initiation of the repair ("other-prompting").

Of course, one has to keep in mind that 26% of the PROPs in self-repairs end in a rising tone, but this does not invalidate the arguments we have just presented. First of all, even if the utterance is first judged to be complete by the speaker, there might be other reasons for the use of a rising tone (attitudinal ones, for instance). Secondly, although the falling tone reinforces the TRP after the PROP, it is not a necessary ingredient, in that the TRP is there irrespective of the tone employed by the speaker; the falling tone merely reinforces the turn-yielding signal. Thirdly, it should be emphasized that we are not dealing with strict rules here, but with tendencies; one should thus not expect perfect mappings of conversational function (repair) and prosodic form (falling tone).

Finally, it should be noted that the intonation of repair-RDs differs significantly from that of some non-repair-RDs, as can be seen in table 6.

Table 6. Intonation of PROP in repair-RDs vs. non-repair-RDs

	repair-RDs	question-RDs
Falling	71	05
Rising	25	06
Total	96	11

This very outspoken difference in distribution strongly suggests that the falling tone in repair-RDs is indeed interactionally relevant; if this was not the case, one would not expect there to be a difference between the different functional types of RD. Whereas the high frequency of falling tones in repair-RDs shows RD to be an interactional process rather than merely a syntactic construction, the higher frequency of rises in one type of non-repair-RDs (questions) supports a less procedural reading. What matters most here is the fact that there *is* a difference, for it suggests a correlation between prosodic form and discourse function. Table 6 thus further supports the interactional evidence of intonation in repair-RDs. We will return to this in chapter 6.

4.3.5. Summary

In this section, we have discussed some prosodic aspects of repair which supply strong, independent evidence in favour of our interactional analysis of repair. First of all, we have argued that that the occurrence of pauses in between PROP and REF is functionally relevant. The pause reflects the speaker's re-organization of his utterance, and may also serve as passive prompting on the part of the hearer that a repair is in order. The fact that PROP and REF are separated by a tone unit boundary also suggests that they are independent functional moves.

Secondly, the intonation, more particularly the final pitch movement on the PROP, of self-repairs was discussed in some detail. The high frequency of falling tones is claimed to be interactionally relevant, in that it signals that the speaker originally regards his utterance as "complete" without the REF. The falling tone is also usually a strong turn-yielding cue; the fact that the hearer does not take advantage of this cue may then be read by the speaker as an indication that a repair is in order.

4.4. Conclusion

In this chapter, we have discussed self-initiated self-repairs, and have shown that they are also evidence in favour of the claim that there is tension in conversation between the Clarity principle and the Economy principle. We have also shown that the process of referent-tracking in conversational discourse is indeed a collaborative *process* in which both speaker and hearer play an active part (see also the findings in Clark—Wilkes-Gibbs 1986; Geluykens 1988b; Geluykens 1993 on referent-introduction). Finally, our findings on the different interactional types of repair provide some evidence for the claim that there may be other types apart from the four major ones distinguished by Schegloff—Jefferson—Sacks (1977).

It remains to be discussed why exactly it is that the anaphors repaired in our data are pragmatically problematic, and give rise to a repair. We will argue, in the following chapter, that this is due to the problematic recoverability status of the reparandum.

We have also not yet gone into the precise nature of the syntactic construction "RD" and its functional status as the reflection of a repair process. We will do this in chapter 6.

Chapter 5

Self-repair and recoverability

5.1. Introduction

In this chapter, we will try to show that the reason why speakers repair their original utterance by means of a REF is due to the problematic recoverability status of the reparandum. That is to say, the inadequate referential status of the reparandum can be understood in terms of its relationship to the preceding discourse context.

As we have pointed out earlier, recoverability depends mainly on inferability, with interference (competing referents) and distance (erosion due to the gap between previous mention of the referent and current mention) as other possible factors. Later on, we will devote some attention to Interference and Distance; for the time being, however, we will be concerned mainly with Inferability. We will offer evidence to show that, in many cases, the referent represented by the reparandum is neither completely irrecoverable ("new") in terms of the previous discourse record, nor completely recoverable ("given"); this is why the reparandum is problematic with respect to the two pragmatic principles (Economy and Clarity) outlined elsewhere. The recoverability status of the gap is actually quite subtle; in fact, a closer investigation of the REF in self-repairs shows that most of the literature on the so-called given-new distinction (as we have already pointed out in chapter 2) leave something to be desired as an analytical tool. This is due to several reasons.

The first reason, as we have already pointed out, is that definitions of given-new —or, in our terms, recoverability— are not sufficiently made operational, and are thus of limited use for data-analysis. The second reason is that it can be shown —and this is in fact what we will do in this chapter— that it makes no sense to talk about a simple binary recoverability distinction. At the very least, what we need is a scale or continuum along which elements can be placed according to the directness of their recoverability. In actual fact, the situation is even more complicated, for what is treated in most DA work as a single, primary notion ("givenness", "thematicity", or whatever term the author might happen to employ), is in fact a complex of different factors (inferability, distance and interference) which, when combined, determine the recoverability status of a referent. Thirdly, and most importantly perhaps, this recoverability status is ultimately an interactional one, in that it is influenced by a number of factors which depend on speaker-hearer interaction, such as the discourse type, the type of activity participants are involved in, the mutually assumed world knowledge, the communicative goals the speaker has in mind, etc. As we have argued in extenso elsewhere (Geluykens 1991a), the informational status of a referent must always be judged against the background of its interactional context. This is why a purely linear, quantitative approach to recoverability has to be ruled out.

This is much more than a theoretical squabble or a matter of choice of theoretical framework; the matter is an empirical issue. If we can show, through our analysis of the data, that we indeed need a complex notion such as recoverability to account for the facts, the claims made above get the status of a testable hypothesis. It is a fault of much of the DA literature that it starts off with an overload of pretheoretical apparatus which is, in most cases, insufficiently based on real data. What we propose to do in fact amounts to the opposite: we start off with as few preconceived ideas as possible, and develop a theoretical framework as we go along. This methodology is inspired more by the CA than by the DA tradition.

Although this study is largely concerned with "information packaging", in that we are dealing with the way reference is maintained, the perspective from which we view this differs from most DA work. In our approach, we show that a purely informational account of a phenomenon does not offer an adequate explanation, since such an approach ignores the interactional dimension of discourse. We are not just saying that information and interaction are, as it were, complementary sides of the same thing. On the contrary, we are saying that, even when language is viewed primarily as information packaging, this is ultimately an interactional phenomenon. In more concrete terms: the analysis of inferablitity offered here is used as supportive evidence for the analysis of RD and related structures in terms of repair. If we restrict ourselves merely to an analysis of REFs in terms of recoverability, we fail to do justice to the procedural nature of the phnomena discussed in this study.

In the following sections, we will pay attention to inferability (5.2), referential distance (5.3), and interference (5.4), respectively.

5.2. Inferability of reference

5.2.1. Inferability through scenario-type semantic links

Let us start off by looking at a relatively straightforward example of a REF which is neither recoverable nor irrecoverable, to illustrate what is meant by inferability [prosodic marking is not included in this chapter]:

(82)   *B: (...) I think her family were vaguely farmers and*
         landowners round about so they knew a lot of
         people and he always hunts - the father does
         (...)   (S.1.13.93.9)

The REF *the father* in (82) has not been mentioned in the preceding context; hence it is not directly recoverable. On the other hand, it is not irrecoverable either, for, in one of the preceding clauses of the same turn, B mentions the referent *her family*. It is part of the "family"-scenario (Sanford—Garrod 1982) —at least in our culture— that families normally consist of a mother, a father and any number of children. Any masculine singular pronoun *he* (such as the reparandum) thus at least has a possibility of being coreferential with the referent *father* in the evoked family-scenario. In other words, there is an element of indirect recoverability.

On the other hand, however, the connection between *family* and the REF *father* is an indirect one, and requires some inferences to be made (plus some knowledge about the organization of the world in general, i.e. knowledge about the existence and organization of the relevant scenario). The speaker cannot automatically assume that the hearer will make the same inferences the speaker himself has just made; the result is that there is a danger of misinterpreted coreference. First of all, the hearer may misinterpret the reference of the gap *he*, and may take it to refer to someone else (based on the same scenario, he may for instance assume that it refers to a brother of the *her* referred to in the context). Secondly, the hearer might be unable to find any plausible referent whatsoever for coreference with *he*.

Whatever the case may be, the speaker realizes that the reference form he has used is communicatively inadequate, and thus in need of repair. This inadequacy arises from the fact that the referent expressed in the REF is neither very recoverable —in which case, following the Economy Principle, a simple pronoun might have sufficed— nor very irrecoverable —in which case, following the Clarity Principle, a full lexical NP would have been used from the outset. The reference is problematic, and requires a number of inferences to be made; this is why we have referred to such referents as inferable information (the term is also used by Prince (1979, 1981), but is used in a different, slightly less restrictive sense here; cf. also Chafe's (1987) "semi-active" label). An inferable referent —or inferable for short— is thus a referent which is neither directly recoverable nor completely irrecoverable, but can be indirectly inferred from the previous discourse record. In (82) above, this inferring is done by virtue of the referent belonging to the same scenario as some other, previously mentioned referent, but, as we will see later on, inferability can be of a different nature.

In (83) below, inferability of the REF is similar to (82), in that the REF has the same "part of"-relationship to some previously mentioned referent:

(83)   A: (...) I got this job in a teacher's training college -
        B: mhm .
        A: which is quite fun I mean <u>they</u>'re not university
              calibre obviously <u>the students</u> on the whole
              but - [∂:m] in some ways they're more fun
              (...) (S.1.6.16.4)

In this example, the REF *the students* is inferable in that it is part of the *college* scenario evoked in A's previous turn: most people know that "colleges have students". On the other hand, the inferential jump the speaker has made from *college* to *students* may be far from obvious to the hearer. In order not to violate the C-principle, the speaker thus judges it safer to repair the pronominal gap they with a full lexical NP (the REF). Note, incidentally, that, whereas (82) has a pause between PROP and REF, this is not the case in (83), despite the comparable inferability status of the two REFs. If there is thus any connection at all between inferability and the occurrence of pauses, it must be a very indirect one.

Note also that the "part of"-relationship between the two referents is such that the REF-referent is usually a lower-order one in the scenario than the previously mentioned referent. For instance, in (83), *students* is inferable from *college*, but this is not necessarily the case the other way round: uttering *students* would not necessarily make a subsequent referent *college* equally inferable. Whereas invoking a "college" automatically implies "a college with students" (it is an essential part of the scenario), the invoking of "students" does not necessarily imply "student of a college"; it might just as well imply "student of a polytechnic", "student on a correspondence course".

5.2.2. Inferability through other semantic links

Inferability through a scenario-type link is the most obvious example of inferable REFs. Most of the time, however, inferability of the REF is less straightforward, in that the link between the REF and the previous discourse record is of a different nature. Consider, for instance, (84):

(84)   A: mhm . [m] well the other garden is not much bigger -
          B: no - ((and it's)) so precious . garden space that [i] is
             for kids (...) (S.4.2.34.7)

In this instance, although the REF *garden space* is clearly related to the previously mentioned referent *the other garden*, this does not make it directly recoverable, as the two referents are *not* identical by any means. Speaker A is talking about a specific, particular "garden", whereas speaker B is referring to the generic "gardens in general"; this shift from specific to generic once again requires an inferential process to be made. The gap *it* in B's original utterance is thus communicatively inadequate, in that it is likely to be interpreted by A as being coreferential with A's *other garden* rather than with B's intended referent *garden space*. In other words, a repair is in order.

Yet another type of inferability can be found in instance (85) below:

(85)   A: *[ə:] where do you go from Hyde Park Corner .*
         B: *well if it's 7 o'clock in the morning I don't see any
                 point in avoiding Knightsbridge ---*
         A: *no ---*
         B: *right . and then I just sit on it -*
         A: *so you go down Park Lane*
         B: *I go down Park Lane and I go round Hyde Park
                 Corner and I hit lots of people going round
                 [ə] Hyde Park Corner . that's the thing which
                 frightens me . is those big roundabouts*
                 (S.4.2.44.7)

The REF *those big roundabouts* is not mentioned explicitly in the
preceding context. Speaker B, however, does mention the referent
Hyde Park Corner. Since A and B are both familiar with London
(they work there), it can be assumed that the fact that there is indeed a
big roundabout at Hyde Park Corner is part of their "mutual
knowledge" (Clark—Marshall 1981). This does not make the REF
directly recoverable, however. First of all, although the speaker can
assume that the hearer is aware of the reference of his reparandum,
he cannot be absolutely sure (this is where factors such as
assumptions about common background, etc. clearly play a part).
Secondly, and more importantly in this case, the speaker makes an
inferential jump from the recoverable *Hyde Park Corner* to one
particular aspect of Hyde Park Corner, viz. the *roundabout* there (in
fact, the link is even more indirect, since the REF is the plural (and
general) *roundabouts* rather than the particular *roundabout* at Hyde
Park Corner; there is thus a similar jump as in (84) from particular to
general). There is no way the speaker can presuppose that the hearer
has made a similar inferential leap (although it is quite possible that
he has), and has interpreted the gap *that* as referring to *those big
roundabouts*, since the inferences to be made here are quite complex.
Put differently: although the speaker has first opted for the E-
principle, and used a pronoun, this probably violates the C-principle,
and thus needs to be repaired.

   Inferability depends on the speaker's judgment about the hearer's
capability to lay an inferential link between a referent (or combination
of referents) and another, following one (the reparandum-referent).
This is clearly to some extent situation-bound, in that it depends on
the relationship between speaker and hearer, on their mutual

knowledge of the world, etc. For someone who does not know anything about London, for instance, the REF *those big roundabouts in* (85) is not at all inferable from the context, but is simply irrecoverable.

In instance (86), the fact that inferability is situation-bound becomes even clearer, since the connection of the REF to the previous discourse is an obscure one for anyone but a specialist in English literature:

(86)   *B: (...) and I've [?] reread Eyeless in Gaza and I am now on [k] Point Counter Point -- [ə:m] - . I've got oh yes that's something else I've got to do before next Tuesday bash on with some James Joyce (...)   (S.7.1.b20.10)*

Inferability of the REF *bash on with some James Joyce* depends on the link between *James Joyce* (part of the REF) and *Aldous Huxley* (who is not even mentioned in the immediately preceding discourse), via the referent *Eyeless in Gaza* (which is explicitly mentioned). A simple pronominalization clearly would not do, as this link is far from obvious. Of course, this is not the only factor which makes a repair necessary. Even assuming that both speaker and hearer in this case are indeed literary specialists (they are to some degree), the REF would still be inferable, since there is no way the hearer could directly predict the inferential leap the speaker has made from *Huxley* to *Joyce* (part of the REF).

In a few cases in the data, the REF is rather directly inferable from the preceding context, which would make it, in more traditional terms, "given" (or, in our terms, directly recoverable). Yet, even here, one sometimes gets a repair, which adds further support to the claim that we are not dealing with a simple binary "given-new" distinction, nor with a purely linear, quantifiable concept. A good example is (87) below:

(87)   *A: (...) --- hasn't some Canadian recently set up a a foundation you're not in fact Canadian though are you*
        B: no .
        A: no -

> *B: no <u>that</u>'s my trouble that was my trouble with*
> > *applying for a Canada Council you see ((and it)) -*
> *A: what*
> *B: I say <u>that</u> was my trouble in [plain in tr] in applying*
> > *for a Canada Council - <u>not being a Canadian</u> *-**
> *A: *yeah**
> *B: citizen you see*
> *A: hm -   (S.2.1.64.4)*

In this exchange, A asks explicitly whether B is Canadian or not. Further on, this information is treated by B as recoverable, and thus pronominalized (hence the gap *that*). However, the referent is clearly not recoverable enough for the hearer, since he indicates that some kind of a repair is in order (cf. *what*). The REF *not being a Canadian* is thus treated as inferable information, and an (other-initiated) repair is created.

Inferability of a referent is like a balance between two factors: communicative efficiency (cf. the E-principle) on the one hand, and unambiguous reference (cf. the C-principle) on the other hand. In (87), the speaker first goes for efficiency, which, given the preceding context, seems a reasonable thing to do, as the gap might be considered recoverable from a purely linear point of view. However, despite this, a trouble-spot occurs, which signals that the speaker has nevertheless overestimates the inferential capacity of the hearer. It is probably not coincidental that the repair is other-initiated rather than self-initiated here, given the fact that inferability can rightly be considered by the speaker to be relatively direct; he therefore sees no immediate need for self-initiating a repair.

In a lot of cases, the reasons for the inferability of the REF are rather less straightforward, and less direct, than in the instances which we have hitherto discussed. A few examples will make this clear:

(88)   *A: because when you've got these two things which*
> > *are . [∂] . essentially alien . being bound up with*
> > *one another one's future - . and . how one learns*
> > *at university - <u>that . that</u> . annoyed me - <u>the</u>*
> > *<u>irrelevance of these two things to each other</u> --*
> > *(S.5.9.35.1)*

In this instance, the REF *the irrelevance...* is derivable from a number of things which are mentioned earlier on in A's turn, viz. *one's future* and *how one does at university*, in combination with the fact that these elements are *alien* to one another. Inferability thus lies in deriving information from a combination of several other pieces of information, and is thus relatively complex and indirect (cf. also the following section).

In (89) below, inferability is of a different type still, depending on near-synonymy:

(89)   *B: besides I was so sick of sitting in Wandsworth Com-*
           mon with mi books that I thought anything to
        A: *(-- laughs) yes*
        B: *get out you know it's lovely* . freedom
           (S.6.2.33.2)

The REF *freedom* is almost synonyous with the previously mentioned *get out*, in that "getting out" of something implies "having freedom" from it. Inferability is thus based on semantic relatedness.

A similar case of indirect inferability is exemplified by instance (90) below, where the REF *the way...* is inferable from the previously mentioned *a kind of donné*, but obviously in a very indirect fashion:

(90)   *a: what about [thi:] kind of situation that begins with*
           Lear . where you get him dividing up his king-
           dom . isn't that equally a kind of donné . *for
           the tragedy*
        A: *yes* it is and [i] it's often been - criticized
           ((the way)) that it's just
        B: **by whom -- by whom**
        A: **. immediately . slipped in -** - [ə:m] ---
           (S.3.5.b44.3)

In this case (and the other ones mentioned so far), although inferability is indirect, at least it derives from a single, identifiable element in the previous context. This is not the case for all inferables, as we will see in the following section.

Before we go into this, let us first turn to one remaining case of inferability which especially merits our attention. Consider (91):

(91)   B: *well what else are we going to get I'm going to get*
        a little sideboard --
        A: *mhm I . think sideboards are the biggest waste of*
        time ever
        B: *you have lots of them - things like them .*
        A: *nhn - I have no sideboards -*
        B: *you need sideboards <u>that</u>'s what your [be] bedroom*
        lacks . is a [b] is <u>a . [ə:] dressing table on which
        there's a mirror</u> and that's essentially what a
        sideboard is - . that is a dressing ta*ble*
        A: **I'm* not going to argue ((on)) things which you're*
        [ə:] totally wrong about   (S.4.2.73.3)

The REF *a dressing table on which there's a mirror* is, at first sight,
irrecoverable, as it is apparently not mentioned in the preceding
discourse context. However, the rest of B's turn after the REF makes
it clear that, for speaker B, the referents *sideboard* and *dressing
table...* can be regarded as being identical, and thus coreferential.
Note that the referent *sideboard(s)*, unlike the REF *a dressing
table...*, is indeed mentioned in the preceding context. This would in
fact make the REF directly recoverable, at least from speaker B's
point of view. However, speaker B cannot be sure that, from hearer
A's point of view, the two above-mentioned referents can be
regarded as coreferential; in fact, from A's final turn it becomes clear
that he disagrees with B on this, and does not regard them as being
coreferential. Speaker B thus cannot treat the REF as recoverable,
since he cannot be sure that speaker A has made the inference
"sideboard equals dressing table"; he therefore assumes —rightly, as
it turns out—, after uttering the PROP, that the reparandum is not
sufficiently recoverable, and thus in need of a repair.
    Instance (91) is further evidence that the traditional DA notions of
given-new are simply inadequate, especially when applied to
conversational data, as they fail to take the interactional dimension
into account. We have shown here that what is recoverable for the
speaker need not be recoverable to the same extent for the hearer (and
vice versa). In each case, one has to make a qualitative appreciation
of what is actually going on between the participants; the final turn of
the exchange in (91) thus confirms our analysis.

5.2.3. Complex inferability

In quite a number of cases, inferability is even less direct, and even harder to pin down, in that it appears to derive not from one particular element (or elements) in the discourse context, but rather from a combination of several factors, or from the context as a whole. The latter is the case, for instance, in (92); in this example, the REF *living in London* derives from the previous conversation, which is concerned with "life in London", as a whole rather than from any single referent or combination of referents. In this respect, it differs from the inferable REFs discussed so far:

(92)   *C: (...) . London is one of the few places . where you*
                have to create your own relaxation . the place
                itself doesn't encourage you
        A: not at all not oh
        *C: quite the reverse *I think**
        *A: *yes* I think it's [∂m] - I think <u>it</u>'s very bad for*
                [∂m] you know your general tone . <u>living in</u>
                <u>*London*</u> *- and not only because of the hurry*
                (...) (S.1.8.61.4)

We will now give two other examples of this kind of indirect inferability, without discussing them in detail:

(93)   *C: (...) the worst thing about my teaching . at the*
                moment Patrick is that on Monday and Tuesday
                afternoon . I take O level . English language
                or English literature . from one fifteen to five
        B: oh
        C: straight through
        B: gosh
        *C: with the same group you know they sit *there**
        *B: *the* same lot*
        C: yep
        B: oh that's cruel isn't it
        *C: I mean they find <u>it</u> a bit off*putting ((you know))* -*
                <u>*coming straight from*</u>
        *B: *yeah**
        *C: **<u>school</u>** and working such *<u>long</u>*

B: **mhm**

C: ((_hours_))*

B: *yes a stretch* like that is all right with something
    practical like making . paper houses but when
    it's [ə:m] . just on book work and so on (...)
    (S.7.1.a31.4)

(94)   B: mhm - but did you not know it was going to be so
        cold and you had no fur gloves and fur hats and
        things with you so nobody died of the cold
    a: no we'd we'd got [klə:] warm clothes with us cos we
        knew . no it was just surprising that
    B: mhm
    C: mhm
    B: mhm
    a: where I say it was a - a dance going on -- . with people
        wearing gloves -
    B: ((no)) James and I came to the conclusion that _that_ was
        why the - English [ə:m] - [ə:m] - rich . upper crust
        had always done so well in life _cos their houses were_
        so bloody cold that that they . not (- coughs)
        (S.1.13.71.4)

In each of these cases, the REF is indirectly inferable from the cited
context, but not from one single element in that context.

5.2.4. Extralinguistic inferability

Finally, let us consider two instances of inferability which are
slightly different from the ones discussed so far:

(95)   [context: A and B looking at series of paintings]
    B: he must count as one of their good pieces
    A: I think it's you know I think it's it good you know
        it's [ə:m]
    B: _it_ affronts me _the way they always paint the hands as_
        something separate (S.1.8.21.3)

(96)   [context: same conversation, further down]

> *A: (...) - so I thought I'd wait till he he had another lot*
> *C: *mhm**
> *A: *I* like <u>that one</u> best - <u>the ((tree)) in the middle</u> - (...)*
>   *(S.1.8.40.1)*

In these instances, the REFs are recoverable from the extralinguistic rather than the linguistic context, the reference being exophoric rather than anaphoric. However, since A and B are looking at a series of paintings rather than a single one, a pronoun does not enable the hearer to identify the intended referent. The REF is thus inferable rather than directly recoverable; hence the repair.

5.3. Referential Distance to antecedent

5.3.1. The non-linear nature of distance

Let us now turn to two other factors which influence the recoverability status of a REF. In this section, we will first consider distance (a term borrowed from Givón 1983; cf. also the discussion in Geluykens 1992, which this section recapitulates).

By distance, as was pointed out in chapter 2, we mean the amount of verbal material intervening between the actual REF and the previous reference to the same referent (in whatever form: full NP, pronoun, etc.). As we have already pointed out, we do not employ the term in the same linear, quantitative sense as Givón (1983) does. We do not think that such a strictly linear approach makes sense; this is all the more true for conversational data. Let us briefly consider why.

In Givón (1983), the factor distance is approached on a strictly quantitative basis: distance of a referent is calculated simply by looking for the previous mention of the same referent (in whatever form, be it full NP, pronoun or zero-anaphor), and counting the number of clauses separating the two occurrences. The upper limit for looking back is, rather arbitrarily, set at 20 clauses to the left (Givón [personal communication] argues that there is some psycholinguistic motivation for this upper limit). Referents are thus given a distance figure somewhere between 1 and 20. This methodology is employed by Givón and his co-workers for analyzing both spoken and written narrative discourse.

This method is unsatisfactory, especially for conversational discourse, for several reasons. First of all, questions may be raised as to the measurement unit, viz. clauses. Conversation is characteristically full of unfinished clauses, false starts, hesitations, pauses, etc. (cf. also Crystal 1980), all of which may have an influence on how distant a referent is judged to be (or, in our terms, on how recoverable a referent is). The turn taking system is a further complicating factor: if a referent has been mentioned, say, five clauses back, it might make a difference whether these clauses all form part of one turn, or whether they belong to five different turns. In spoken language, the speech rate may also affect the recoverability status of a referent. On top of that, one has to take into account the fact that there is always more than one participant in conversation; it may therefore make a difference whether the previous mention of a referent is done by the same speaker, or by a different speaker.

Secondly, the degree of recoverability of a referent will depend to a much larger degree on the nature of the intervening material than on its sheer quantity. For instance, if there is a side sequence (Jefferson 1972) between two mentions of the same referent, this will create complications. An example from our data will make this clear; consider example (97) below:

(97)   A: *yes I see . yes . yes - [∂:m] . one other thing Sam -*
           [∂:m] - Delaney - a Canadian *((who)) graduated -*
        B: **(([∂:] where did you* put those things just one)) .*
           let me put this in my bag ((or)) I'll ((walk away
           without it)) ---
        A: *[∂:m] --- Delaney's the Canadian . student remember*
           last year
        B: *mhm*
        A: *(...) (S.1.1.5.2) (cf. also Geluykens 1992)*

In purely quantitative terms, about three clauses separate the two mentions of *Delaney* in the first and third turn, respectively. However, these three clauses in B's turn constitute a side sequence (Jefferson 1972: they are concerned with something completely different, and are not related to what A is trying to talk about; B, as it were, puts A's referent temporarily "on the shelf". Compare this to the (constructed) exchange in (98) (cf. Geluykens 1992) :

(98)   A: (...) - _Delaney_
         B: oh yes I remember . it all comes back to me now -
             yeah sure do go on .
         A: _Delaney_ (...)

There is the same number of clauses intervening here. However, since the intervening material is of a completely different nature, it would be reasonable to assume that the recoverability status of _Delaney_ in (98) differs from that in (97). In other words: it is not merely the quantity of the intervening material which is important, but also, and more so, its quality. In narrative discourse, these problems are of course not as outspoken (although, even in that discourse type, there might be an interactional dimension); in conversation, however, they show the inadequacies of a purely quantitative approach to information flow.

A third criticism that can be raised against Givón (1983) concerns the amount of preceding material one has to take into consideration for determining recoverability. His upper limit is, as we have argued, rather arbitrary. First of all, there is no real reason for not looking even further back (the objections that can be raised against this are more of a practical nature). Secondly, one may wonder whether one has to go back as far as 20 clauses in all cases. The latter question is especially pertinent for conversational discourse, which is of a totally different nature than narrative discourse.

We do not think the upper limit proposed by Givón (1983), or any other strict upper limit for that matter, can be applied straightforwardly to conversation. Some reasons for this have already been mentioned, but there are others. In narratives, the development of the discourse is much more linear than in conversation: one does not introduce referents (e.g. characters) unless they are needed for the progression of the story-line, etc. Furthermore, the interactional dimension is less outspoken. This is not the case to the same extent in conversation, in which participants switch more easily from one topic —we use the term in a non-technical sense here— to the next. Since there is no prior planning, and since the development of the discourse depends on at least two participants, there is not the same amount of linearity in conversation.

All this might imply that, if there is an upper limit for recoverability in conversation, this upper limit is likely to be less than the one proposed for narratives. Indeed, although there are exceptions, conversation on the whole seems to operate on a more local level. However, we raise the more serious issue here of whether such an upper limit is at all posssible, rather than at which point it should be drawn. In practice, we will indeed concentrate on only a small amount of the preceding discourse. It is important to realize, though, that we will let circumstances determine how far we go back. This is not due to arbitrariness on our part, but is inspired by the insight that is is impossible to approach recoverability on a purely quantitative basis. If this makes our approach appear less rigorous than the one advocated by Givón (1983), this is because we want to avoid oversimplification.

5.3.2. Referential distance and self-repairs

All this being said, let us become a bit more concrete. In all our examples of inferability, the information from which the REF can be inferred is present in the context which immediately precedes the REF. Indeed, when a referent has been mentioned, say, in the immediately preceding turn, it is clear that recoverability will be very direct (always assuming there are no interactional factors disturbing this!); e.g.:

(99)   A: *have you seen* Steve *lately?*
        B: *Yeah - I talked to* him *yesterday.*

Imagine, however, a large amount of linguistic material intervening between *Steve* and *him;* recoverability of the referent would then be far from obvious. In fact, it is reasonable to assume that recoverability "erodes" after a while. Roughly speaking, one would say that the more material intervenes, the less recoverable a referent will become. However, we also claim (cf. above) the nature of the intervening material to be relevant in this respect; this makes distance inherently unquantifiable.

Eventually, depending on a number of factors, the two mentions of a referent will become so distant that the referent (i.e. its second mention) will become irrecoverable again. On becoming more distant, referents will thus pass through a stage where they are neither directly recoverable nor completely irrecoverable. They will thus have a status which is comparable to inferable status, and sometimes give rise to repairs, due to the clash between the Clarity principle and the Economy principle.

It must be pointed out, though, that inferability and distance are independent factors; compare, for instance:

(100)   *I have a job in a college.*
         They're not university calibre, the students.

(101)   *I have a job in a college.*
         [10 intervening turns]
         They're not university calibre, the students.

In (100), the referent *the students* is inferable, as it is recoverable only indirectly from the preceding context; it is not distant, however. In (101), on the other hand, *the students* is both inferable and distant, as there is a lot of intervening material (the nature of which we will leave open here). This shows that the two factors are independently variable. We will indeed come across some cases where both inferability and distance play a part.

Instance (102) below is a clear example of a distant REF, represented here with all the intervening material:

(102)   *B: (...) that's nine years -*
         A: mhm ((it's)) a long time
         B: ((I know it's)) a long time and the house ((would)) be
             much more valuable by that time -
         A: a long time to live in a grotty house isn't it .
         B: but it won't be a grotty house if it's all done up you
             silly twit
         A: (- laughs) -- mhm
         B: be a nice house you keep saying if the money was
             spent on it it'd be a nice house
         A: yeah that's ((allright)) I I just *don't think*
         B: *but* <u>that</u>'s why it's worth spending money on it .
             <u>*because you're likely to live there for - [ə:] maximally*</u>
             <u>*nine years*</u> *. grant you *.**
         A: *(. voiced sigh)*
         B: maximally - I don't want much more (...) (S.4.2.39.3)

In this example, seven turns intervene between the REF *because ... nine years* and the previously mentioned *nine years* (cf. the first turn of the exchange). Although the intervening material is all related, in that it is all on the same topic, this clearly makes the REF distant, and thus problematic in terms of recoverability when it is pronominalized. Hence the repair. Moreover, the REF is also inferable, since only part of it is directly recoverable (i.c. *nine years*); this shows again that inferability and distance can occur together. The following is a comparable instance, given in an abbreviated format:

(103)   *A: do you want people to come to the registry office -*
             [10 turns, ca. 15 tone units intervening, in
             [which "registry office" is not mentioned, but
             [which deal with "invitations to a wedding"
         B: but it's . [ush] you know it's a . waste of time going to a
         *registry office *((2 sylls))* (S.7.3.f55.4)*

Once again, the intervening material is related to the referents under discussion.

Instance (104) is interesting, as the intervening material is qualitatively different; the telephone conversation inserted between the two mentions is a long side sequence (Jefferson 1972). Immediately after the side sequence, A uses a RD to refer to the REF *recognized teacher in applied linguistics:*

(104)   *A: well he certainly can't be a reader - [ə:] otherwise they*
             *wouldn't be asking for recog*nition* -- [ə:m] ---*
         *B: *no**
         A: ((2 or 3 sylls)) not sure what his status is . certainly
             [ə:m] .my evidence for saying that he was a lecturer
             falls to the ground because that was the previous job --
             *[ə:] lecturer *at the University* of Byfleet*
         *B: *mhm**
         A: [Telephone Conversation, lasting about 25 tone units,
             between A and a third party, intervenes]
         A: thank you (replaces receiver) --- [ə:m] -- well --- [ə:m] --
             [?i] you know this this this struck me as a kind of
             *odd title *. you see**
         *B: *mhm - mhm**
         *A: . [ə] recognized teacher **in applied linguistics***

> B: **mhm . mhm**
> A: - [ə] . you know with applied in brackets (...)
>   (S.1.2.a5.13)

This once again shows that it makes no sense to approach the factor distance from a purely quantitative point of view. In (104), it is the nature of the intervening material rather than its quantity (the telephone conversation is not that long, from the point of view of time elapsed) which makes recoverability of the reparandum-referent problematic. Once again, the REF in (104) is inferable as well as distant.

5.4. Interference

Finally, let us consider the third factor which influences the recoverability status of referents, viz. interference, i.e. the existence of other plausible candidates for coreference. In such cases, the problematic recoverability is not strictly speaking due to a cognitive constraint, i.e. the limited capacity of the hearer's consciousness, or its ability to make inferences, but solely to factors in the surrounding context.

We can best make interference clear by means of a concrete example from our data:

(105)   [context: about finding good location for course]
         B: [ə:] if not Imola Cyprus - which is once again I think
               having a bit of an up and up - [ə:m] under Craig de
               Leon I may be *wrong*
         A: *yes* . yes . I [kwai] I quite agree there
         B: I think this is a possibility *.*
         A: *yes*
         B: [ə:m] - or [ə:m] - just possibly Rimini ((it's a bit small
               scale I think [?] Rimini (...) (S.1.2.38.13)

Note, first of all, that the REF Rimini can hardly be labelled inferable, since it is directly retrievable from the immediately preceding clause in B's turn. Secondly, the antecedent of the pronominal gap can hardly be less distant, as there is no intervening linguistic material whatsoever. Note, however, that in the immediately preceding context, there is not one but three possible candidates for coreference with the reparandum *it*. Not only do we get the intended referent *Rimini* in B's repair turn, in a previous turn B also mentions the referents *Imola* and *Cyprus*. Although *Rimini* is the least distant referent, the speaker nevertheless cannot be sure that the hearer will not read either of the other two referents as being coreferential with *it*. Once again, then, the REF has a problematic recoverability status, not because of inferability or distance, but because of interference from other potential co-referents.

The term interference is used in more or less the same sense here as in Givón (1983), from where it is borrowed. Note that, for referents to interfere, they ought to have the same number and gender as the intended referent. They must also be "semantically plausible", in the sense that the resulting proposition would make sense if the pronoun (reparandum) were read as being coreferential with one of the interfering referents. For instance, in (105), the referent *possibility* could, strictly speaking, be coreferent with the reparandum, but it is unlikely to interfere, as the proposition "the possibility is a bit small scale" is unlikely to come to the hearer's mind as a possible reading in this particular context.

Interference is a factor which is largely independent both from inferability and from distance. One could, for instance, imagine a context in which the potential candidates for coreference with the reparandum are not directly recoverable, as in (105), but are all indirectly inferable from the context; there might even be a mixture of directly and indirectly recoverable interfering referents. It seems likely in such cases, however, that referents which are only indirectly recoverable will be less likely to interfere with directly recoverable referents. For instance, in the following example, the inferable referent *the students* (which is inferable by virtue of belonging to the *college* -scenario) does not really interfere with the intended antecedent *my colleagues;* the speaker can thus safely pronominalize:

(106)   *I've got this job in a teacher's training college; my col-*
        leagues aren't very nice. They're not terribly bright either.

There is also probably some correlation with distance, in that the more distant a competing referent is, the less likely the chance of it interfering as a potential co-referent for the gap. Note, however, that there is no strict quantitative rule for this; in the *Rimini* example

(105), to name but one case in point, the intended antecedent is the last mentioned of the possible candidates, but nevertheless suffers from interference from two more distant (in terms of the amount of intervening material) referents.

5.5. Conclusion

In this chapter, we have attempted to show that the reasons for the use of RD and related phenomena as a repair mechanism must be sought in the problematic recoverability status of the pronominal referent.

In most cases, the intended referent is inferable from the preceding discourse record rather than being directly recoverable or completely irrecoverable. This results in a clash between the E-principle (favouring a pronominal form) and the C-principle (favouring a full NP), in its turn resulting in a subsequent repair process (often realized as a RD). Two other factors can make recoverability problematic, viz. distance from the previous mention of the referent, and interference from other referents.

Altough these three factors may be labelled "informational", in that they deal with the interpretation of referential information by speakers and hearers, the problem is, ultimately, an interactional one, in that it depends crucially on the immediate interactive collaboration between speaker and hearer, and on the way speakers assess hearers' capabilities to recover reference from the context.

Chapter 6

Right-dislocation and self-repair

6.1. Preliminaries

6.1.1. Introduction and outline

In this chapter, we will go into the syntactic repercussions of our findings on self-repair in chapters 3 and 4. We have already pointed out that the outcome of many of the self-initiated self-repair processes in chapter 3 can be considered to be, from a syntactic point of view, a "right-dislocation" (RD for short). If this is indeed the case, that would mean that the syntactic construction RD —or at least a subset of it— is in fact the direct reflection of an interactional process, i.c. that of anaphor (self-)repair.

Several points will be made in this chapter. First of all, in section 6.2, we will attempt to show that the self-repair processes discussed in the previous chapters can indeed be considered to fall under the syntactic heading "RD". Secondly, it will be argued that the syntactic category of RD defies strict categorization. In section 6.3, we will consider instances of self-repair which, from a grammatical point of view, may or may not be considered to be RDs, depending on where one draws the boundary between what qualifies as a RD and what does not. We thus show the syntactic category RD to exhibit prototypical organization (see Lakoff 1987). Thirdly, and arguably most importantly, we will go a bit deeper into the relationship between the syntactic category RD and its possible discourse functions (one of them being self-repair). We will show that there is no one-to-one correspondence between syntactic form and discourse function, as at least two other functions of RD can be distinguished. We will also show that there are important interactional and prosodic differences between the self-repair function of RD and its other functions; by doing so, we will provide indirect evidence in favour of our analysis of RDs in terms of self-repair in the previous chapters.

6.1.2. Formal characterization of RD

In order to be able to identify instances of RD, and related constructions, in our database, we need an operational characterization of the phenomenon. As a starting-point, let us look at a recent description of RD, viz. the one in Quirk et al. (1985), who label RD "postponed identification" (Quirk et al. 1985: 1310), and describe it as involving "placing a pro-form earlier in the sentence while the noun phrase to which it refers is placed finally as an amplificatory tag". The example they give is similar to our canonical example in chapter 1:

(107)   *He's a complete idiot, that brother of yours.*

The authors also point out that the operator may be included with the noun phrase, sometimes with inversion:

(108)   *It went on far too long, your game did.*

(109)   *He's a complete idiot, John is/is John.*

If we take this characterization as our starting-point, we can say that RDs consist of a sentence with a pro-form, followed by a noun phrase which has the same reference as the preceding pronoun. Before we proceed any further, we will first introduce some terminology for the basic parts of RD; this will also make clear why we have chosen some of our labels in earlier chapters. The NP following the main clause we will label the Referent (REF for short). The main clause itself will be labelled the Proposition (or PROP). The pronominal element in the proposition, finally, will be labelled the Gap.

We can consider cases such as the ones mentioned in (107-109) to be prototypical RD's, which can be schematically represented as (110):

(110)   Proposition + Referent.

However, we clearly need a more detailed description. We will attempt to show that a formal —in the sense of strict syntactic— description will not suffice, and that RD can only be adequately characterized on a semantic level. Moreover, we will argue that the RD phenomenon has prototypical organization, both on a semantic and on a syntactic level. Also, we will show that on a functional, interactional level, no clear distinction can be drawn between RD and related repair phenomena.

As a first syntactic approximation, we can say that RDs are combinations of a complete Clause —"complete" in the sense that all the argument slots of the verbal predicate are filled— and a "bare" NP, i.e. an NP which is not the argument in another clause.

Clearly, this will not do. We will argue that a characterization of RD only makes sense in semantic rather than syntactic terms. First of all, the major relationship between the REF and the gap, viz. that of coreferentiality, is semantic in nature. Secondly, only a semantic account will enable us to arrive at a level of generality where it is possible to ignore superficial syntactic differences, such as between (107) and (108-109) in the previous section. When we talk about RD as a "construction", then, this has to be understood in the following manner: they are constructions in the sense that they form a specific combination of certain semantic properties (naturally, in combination with their linear properties, i.e. the relative order of the relative parts).

Semantically, the most important characteristic of RD is the particular relationship between the gap and the REF. First of all, the gap and the REF can be said to be coreferential. Put differently: one of the argument-slots in the PROP (i.e. the gap) is a pronominal element, and this element is semantically co-indexed with the non-argument NP immediately following it (i.e. the REF). Furthermore, there is an (backwards) anaphora relationship between gap and REF. By this we mean the following. Of the two elements involved, the gap is semantically general, whereas the REF is semantically specific. Since they refer to the same referents, we can say that the gap in RDs is cataphoric, since it refers forward to the following, specific REF.

The gap is usually one of the core arguments of the PROP; for instance, in a two-place predicate it can be subject, as in (111), or object, as in (112):

(111)   *He likes beans, Steve.*

(112)   *Steve likes them, beans.*

This means that, as far as semantic case-roles are concerned, the REF/gap-referent will usually be either the Agent or the Patient case role. It appears, however, that the gap can also be one of the more oblique cases, such as a locative:

(113)   *Steve put the beans there, in this cupboard.*

The gap can even be part of an argument, for instance of the subject in (114), and of the object in (115):

(114)   *His mother likes beans, Steve's.*

(115)   *I like his mother, Steve's.*

Note that the RD-REF's in (113) to (115) appear to be case-marked.

Cases like the ones mentioned above constitute what we will call prototype RDs; we can represent them schematically in the following manner:

(116)   syntax: [clause with pro-form$_i$]   [NP$_i$]
        semantics: [prop. with general form]   [specific form]
        terminology: [PROP with gap]   [REF]

As for the types of constituent which can appear as the REF, we have so far only discussed instances of NPs. However, other types of constituent can also appear as the REF; an obvious alternative are PPs, as in (113) above. A semantic, prototypical definition of RD allows us to generalize quite easily over NP-REFs and PP-REFs. Other types of constituent can appear as the REF (as we will see in section 6.3.), an example being gerundial forms:

(117)   *Steve likes that, eating beans.*

Going one step further, infinitival clauses can also appear as REFs:

(118)   *Steve likes that, to eat beans.*

Once again, a prototype characterization allows us to consider these simply as RDs, rather than as different constructions. Note, incidentally, that instances such as (12) are problematic, in that they are structurally very similar to so-called Extrapositions (Ross 1967); the latter are exemplified by (119) below:

(119)   *It is easy to eat beans.*

We will return to this problem later on.

There are certain cases for which, from a strict syntactic point of view, the construction might fail to meet the criteria to qualify as a RD, but which are semantically very similar to our prototype cases. Once again, we will regard these as being RDs on semantic grounds. Our functional analysis will provide further justification for doing so. The cases are of two types.

A first case we have already mentioned. It was pointed out earlier that Quirk et al. (1985) regard instances such as (108) as being RDs:

(108) It went on far too long, your game did.

Indeed, though syntactically speaking (2) differs from (120) below, the semantic similarity is so striking that we will regard them as being essentially the same construction:

(120)   *It went on far too long, your game.*

Note that the repetition of the operator in such RDs can also occur with inversion, witness (121):

(121)   *He likes beans, does Steve.*

A second case of less prototypical RDs has to do with the fact that RD typically occurs in informal spoken discourse. As a result, one gets data such as the following:

(122)   *He likes beans, Steve I mean.*

On a purely syntactic reading, these would probably not qualify as RDs. However, it seems clear that the addition of *I mean* does not fundamentally alter the status of the construction in (122): semantically, it is identical to the prototypical version. Once again, one needs a higher level of generality.

In our characterization of RD so far, the prime criterion is thus semantic in nature: the relationship between the REF and gap is essential for a construction to qualify as a RD.

There are a few additional operational criteria which one has to take into account if one wants to characterize RDs; these criteria are due to the fact that we are dealing with conversational discourse. This fact creates three problems which have to be resolved if we want to identify RDs on a systematic basis.

The first of the additional criteria has to do with speech acts (Searle 1969). Up to now, we have only discussed declarative RDs, which will usually function as statements in actual discourse. However, it is clear that RDs could have other illocutionary forces. Specifically, we will encounter instances in which RDs function as a question, usually a yes-no-question:

(123)   *Is that what it really is about, a cock and a fox?*

(This is an actual, slightly simplified example from our database.) Although the majority of RDs in our database are indeed statements, we have to be aware of the fact that other speech acts do occur, and that they may have very specific discourse functions (apart from their speech act status).

The second aspect has to do with the interactional nature of conversation, i.e. with the fact that there is always more than one participant involved. Up to now, we have taken for granted that the entire RD is uttered by one and the same speaker (due to it being a self-repair). However, we have to take into account that this need not always be the case in dialogues; instances such as (124) might well occur:

(124)   A: *he likes beans.* (PROP)
         B: *this guy Steve does.* (REF)

We will also discuss instances such as (18) in detail in chapter 7; for the time being, it suffices to point out that they are functionally very similar to RDs.

Thirdly, and finally, we will discuss problems arising from the turn-taking nature of conversation (cf. Sacks—Schegloff—Jefferson 1974). The PROP and the REF of RDs might be in different turns, as in (125), which is a slightly simplified example from our database:

(125)   A: *that would be rather uncommon.*
          B: *what?*
          A: *to have no food taboos and so forth.*

There is no apriori reason for excluding such cases (which are in fact the other-initiated self-repairs discussed in chapter 3) as non-central instantiations of RD. In fact, we have seen that instances like (125) are quite a common conversational strategy.

One might argue in favour of a scale for RDs, ranging from cases in which the structural link between REF and PROP is a very tight one, to cases in which there is some structural boundary between the two. Such a boundary might be an intervening turn, but also a pause, or a tone group boundary (since we are dealing with spoken discourse, punctuation does not enter into the picture). Note that, although we refer to prosody here, we make no apriori claims about its function in discourse.

Summing up: we have argued in favour of a prototype characterization of RDs; a strictly categorial account, which might work for the prototype cases, does not allow us to make sufficient generalizations over superficially slightly different instances. On top of such a semantic definition, we need a few criteria arising from the conversational nature of the database.

6.2. RD as the reflection of conversational repair

When we turn towards the self-initiated self-repair data, it becomes obvious that quite a number of cases, from a formal point of view, meet the criteria for RD outlined in the previous section. Starting with the central cases of RD, let us consider some instances of self-repair which are concatenations of a PROP and a subsequent bare NP (all instances of RD are underlined):

(126)   A: *(...) it's /quite `bitter # / `'Guinness I think #*
          (S.1.7.36.7)

(127)   B: *yes . yes they're /damned `tricky   those 'little 'roads # --*
          you know the sort of thing   (S.1.11.b79.2)

(128) *B: (...) --- I /think <u>it's a bit of [əmə] . an a`malgam</u> #*
       ((/<u>this `map</u> #)) (S.2.3.8.6)

(129) *c: ((1 syll)) /<u>these were `made all - in the `thirties</u> #*
       <u>these par`ticular `films</u> # (S.4.4.103.5)

(130) *B: well /<u>they were `more like `sermons</u> # <u>his /`lectures</u> # he*
       just pounded (S.5.9.79.5)

Apart from the fact that these RDs have an NP as their REF, none of them has a pause intervening between PROP and REF. There are, of course, also a lot of RDs which do have a pause between PROP and NP-REF; e.g.:

(131) *A: /well <u>it's a `jolly `nice `place</u> # - <u>the /new uni-versity</u> #*
       (S.1.10.56.1)

(132) *B: (...) they /come [`back] with a `blue `pencil # - <u>a /lot of</u>*
       <u>the `good bits</u> # (S.3.6.49.2)

(133) *c: [ə:m] . ((2 sylls)) - I /think <u>it looks as `though it `works</u>*
       <u>very `well</u> # - <u>their /method of . `repro`duction</u> # -
       (S.4.4.36.3)

(134) *A: I /like `'that one `best # - <u>the /((tree)) in the `middle</u> # -*
       but I think it's too [ə:] it would dominate the room
       a bit too much (S.1.8.40.1)

(135) *A: (...) /<u>that . an`noyed me</u> # - <u>the ir/`relevance # of /these</u>*
       <u>`two [`things] to each `other</u> # -- (S.5.9.35.1)

Finally, there are some instances of RDs with an NP-REF which have a turn intervening between the PROP and the REF; e.g.:

(136) *B: and be/sides <u>she always `comes `down [in the</u>*
       <u>/`summer</u> #] #
       *c: your sister *. or your mother**
       *B: *[ə:] <u>my /sister and</u>* my `mother # . /both of them #*
       (S.1.12.122.6)

This is of course an instance of other-initiated self-repair. Note the lack of agreement in number between the gap and the REF.

As far as other types of constituent are concerned, there are some instances in the data which have a PP as their REF; e.g.:

(137)   A: *have /you been 'listening to that as 'well # /-to [∂:] # the the /Cold 'Comfort `'Farm ((and all 'that)) #* (S.2.8.b39.5)

(138)   D: *we /used to 'have the 'library `here # you see 'chairman # . ((/under [thi:] . 'wing where . geography 'has its big* - it smelled of mice (...) (S.3.4.91.1)

Other types of constituent which can occur as the REF, and which give rise to non-prototypical RDs, will be discussed in the following section.

As cases of RD which are non-central, in that the REF is not really a non-argument NP, we should mention instances such as (139-140):

(139)   B: (...) *and /he 'always `hunts # - the /`father `does # and the "/`daughter 'does* # (...) (S.1.13.93.9)

(140)   B: (...) . */that's the thing which `frightens me # . is /those big `roundabouts* # (S.4.2.44.7)

In both these cases, we get a periphrastic verb accompanying the REF, functioning as a pro-form for the main verb of the PROP.

To finish our discussion of fairly central RDs, we should mention a few instances of self-repair which do not really qualify as RDs anymore from a formal point of view:

(141)   A: yeah # . well *he's /got a [`very good 'bloke] doing it `'now # . I /-mean # . /doing this `'organizing* # (...) (S.5.11.a35.2)

(142)   B: [∂] */I'm typing it 'up `now # . /typing up the final*
A: [hm]
B: *`copy* # (S.2.1.1.6)

In both these instances, the main verb of the original utterance is repeated, and the "REF" thus cannot be said to be a bare NP. In some cases, we even get repetition of both the verb and the subject; e.g.:

(143)   A: *but /this is something I `want # /one day I want a*
        `room # where a / `sewing machine # /stands `up #
        /`permanently # (S.1.3.12.11)

We will return to instances like (141-143) in chapter 8. For the time being, it suffices to note that they are structurally rather far removed from "core" RDs, to the point where the label RD seems inappropriate.

6.3. Prototype organization: non-prototypical RDs

6.3.1. Preliminaries

In this section, we will be concerned with patterns which still qualify as RDs, but which are less central than the RDs discussed so far. In the RDs discussed up to now, the REF represents a single referent, realized usually by an NP, sometimes by a PP. There are cases, however, where the gap is a substitute for an entire state-of-affairs rather than a single referent; the REF then expresses an entire proposition in its own right, realized as a kind of non-argument subordinate clause. In what follows, we will discuss some types of non-prototypical RDs, classified according to the form of the REF. Before we embark on this, however, let us consider a straightforward example from the data, which was already discussed in an earlier section:

(144)   B: *no that's my trouble that was my trouble with applying*
        for a Canada Council you see ((and it)) -
        A: *what*
        B: *I say that was my trouble in [plain in tr] in applying for*
        a Canada Council - not being a Canadian *-*
        A: **yeah**
        B: *citizen you see*
        A: *hm - (S.2.1.64.4)*

The REF *not being a Canadian citizen* represents an entire proposition rather than a single referent; despite this, the same repair process is at work here as in the RDs with NP-REFs. That is why we also consider these constructions to be RDs, albeit less prototypical ones from a syntactic point of view.

Including patterns of the type [PROP + clausal REF] as RDs does create problems, however, for there are constructions which are semantically very similar in structure, but which cannot be labelled RDs. The phenomenon we are referring to here is that of "extraposition" (Ross 1967); e.g.:

(145)   *It is easy being a Canadian.*

(146)   *It is easy to be a Canadian.*

Extraposition has to be distinguished from RD, for several reasons. First of all, contrary to RD, extraposition is not always a matter of free choice on the part of the speaker: some extrapositions are obligatory, as is shown by the ungrammaticality of (148) as opposed to (147):

(147)   *It seems that John is Canadian.*

(148)   **That John is Canadian seems.*

Furthermore, the function of extraposition seems to differ radically from that of RD. First of all, it is claimed in the literature (e.g. Creider 1979) that extraposition is used to put an entire sub-clause "in focus" at the end of the utterance. There also appear to be sheer structural reasons for the use of extraposition, in that it puts a constituent which is structurally "heavy" —viz. a sub-clause— towards the right of the utterance. This is labelled the end-weight principle by Quirk et al. (1985); Dik (1978) claims this to be due to the universal LIPOC (or Language-Independent Position for the Order of Constituents) principle. At any rate, RD seems to differ fundamentally from extraposition, in that in the latter case the pattern is clearly planned in advance, either for structural reasons (LIPOC, end-weight), or for information packaging ones (end-focus), or both; in RDs, on the other hand, the pattern emerges interactionally as the discourse unfolds, and is unplanned.

The problem is that, without taking functional considerations into account from the outset, RD and extraposition are hard to differentiate. Both involve a proposition with a pronominal gap, which is followed by a clausal REF. The only formal criterion seems to be that the "gap" in extrapositions is always realized as *it*; whenever this is not the case, chances thus are that we are dealing with a RD. This does not solve the entire problem, however, since there are instances in the data with an *it*-gap which can only be considered to be RDs, as they have to be interpreted in terms of repair. In some cases, the occurrence of a pause, or the prosodic shape, can be an indicator, though never conclusive evidence, for regarding a construction as a RD rather than as an extraposition. In the end, however, since we are dealing here with the fuzzy borderline between what can still be considered to be a RD and what not, we have to take functional considerations into account, such as the fact whether the pattern is clearly an unplanned repair or not.

With these provisos in mind, we can start looking at the data. We have distinguished three types of clausal-REF-RDs: those with a gerundial REF, those in which the REF is a non-finite sub-clause, and those in which the REF is a finite sub-clause. As a fourth type, we will discuss RDs where the PROP has the form of an inverted pseudo-cleft utterance (or iPSC for short), and which also have a clausal REF.

6.3.2. RDs with gerundial REF

There are 34 instances of these in the data. Instance (38) in the previous section in fact belongs in this category; it is the only instance of an other-initiated repair with a gerundial REF.

Most RDs of this type are self-initiated; some of them have a pause between PROP and REF, just like the ones discussed in chapter 3; e.g.:

(149)   A: (...) but I /found <u>it</u> so "very `difficult # . / `working in the `day # . and /trying to 'study (...) # (S.3.1.c5.2)

(150)   A: (...) <u>it's</u> /very ex`pensive # . / `running this `system # . you / `see # (...) (S.2.2.a134.6)

(151)   *A: yes I /think it's [∂:m] - I /think it's very "∧bad for [∂:m]*
          you /know your general `'tone . [/living in `London #]
          # (...) (S.1.8.61.4)

Other RDs in the data have no pause between PROP and REF; e.g.:

(152)   *A: (...) be/cause it's been [∂?] terrible lugging `Karl a'bout*
          # /`'you know # (S.1.10.64.4)

(153)   *A: (...) . and it was /quite `sweet 'actually # /watching these*
          'young `children # . [∂:] /`learning `this # - and I got
          quite fond of them actually (S.5.9.50.2)

It should be pointed out that some of these could be interpreted as
planned instances, adhering to the end-weight principle, rather than
as real repairs.

6.3.3. RDs with non-finite sub-clausal REF

The propositional REF in non-prototype RDs can also be expressed
by a non-finite sub-clause. In, most cases, we are dealing with a *to*
-infinitive; e.g.:

(154)   *A: /well that `is 'hard 'work #*
          B: (- coughs) and [∂:]
          A: to /keep the 'kids 'quiet ((for an 'after`noon))
          (S.1.7.70.1)

(155)   *A: (...) he /said that he thought this might be `difficult # . to*
          /`climb 'up `there # - (S.4.2.4.3)

In a few instances, the REF consists of a bare infinitive clause; e.g.:

(156)   *B: and I've [?] reread Eyeless in Gaza and I am now on [k]*
          Point Counter . Point -- [∂:m] - . I've got oh yes #
          that's /something else I've 'got to 'do before next
          `Tuesday # /bash on with some James `Joyce #
          (...) (S.7.1.b20.10)

It appears that these patterns cannot be considered extrapositions, but are instances of RD; the fact that the gap consists of *this* or *that* rather than *it* is additional evidence for this.

6.3.4. RDs with finite sub-clausal REF

The majority of clausal REFs consists of a finite sub-clause. Mostly, the REF is a *that* -clause; some examples:

(157)   A: *yes and there's no need everybody comes to *London**
        B: **I know**
        A: */this is the 'very [ə:m] /this'll /obviously is the `bad*
            'thing about 'living in 'London # that - one /doesn't
            travel e'nough to [`see 'other] `'people # . one
            always expects them to come to one (S.1.9.13.3)

(158)   B: *yes --- good # --- /that's `good then # that /you got up*
            and asked a 'question # because he would sort of be
            aware that . you existed (S.2.5.a23.5)

In a minority of cases, the REF is something else than a *that* -clause, for instance a *because* -clause expressing an adverbial of reason, as in (159):

(159)   B: *which nobody bothers to get rid of --- I /mean they*
            main`'tain # . that they lost /`China [be/cause of
            -this #] # --- because /Truman was being ad`'vised
            # /by a very high 'ranking # /State De'partment
            `communist # (S.2.1.b1.2)

All these are clear RDs rather than extrapositions; apart from the non-occurrence of *it* as gap, this is also corroborated by the regular occurrence of a pause between PROP and REF.

6.3.5. RDs with an iPSC-type PROP

There are quite a few cases where the PROP of the RD is an inverted pseudo-cleft sentence (or iPSC); iPSCs have the following form:

(160)   *This is what I've done.*

In other words, an iPSC is a pseudo-cleft in which the order of the *wh*-clause and the other element are inverted; this other element, incidentally, need not be a pronoun (although in RDs this is of course always the case, it being the gap), but can also be a full lexical NP:

(161)   *A book is what I read.*

For a full discussion of iPSCs in the context of their information packaging function, we refer the reader to Geluykens (1988a).

As a first example of an iPSC-RD, consider (162), in which the REF is a non-finite sub-clause:

(162)   *B: oh so you're having a sort of course A and - *one
          and three*
          A: *well # [`this] is 'what `Rivens* `wanted # to /intro'duce
          'course "`one into Rufford # well (S.1.9.67.7)*

In most iPSCs, however, the REF is a finite sub-clause expressing an adverbial of reason; e.g.:

(163)   *B: ((no)) "/James and I 'came to the con´clusion # that /that
          was `why the # - /English [ə:m] - [ə:m] - 'rich . [?]
          upper 'crust # had /always `done so 'well in 'life # cos
          their /`houses were so 'bloody 'cold # (...)
          (S.1.13.71.4)*

(164)   *A: but /this is 'why I asked that `question # ((cos)) /I was
          quite con"`vinced # /I'd [s] I'd 'find [`Gordon] sort
          of [`busily] plastering 'up the ``garage # (...)
          (S.2.10.122.5)*

One step further removed from central RDs are iPSC with a REF which is a complete, independent clause in its own right, such as (165):

(165)   *A: /actually that's what `I do # /I "`buy 'books # and /leave
          them a`round # . to im/`press 'people # (S.2.10.49.6)*

In such instances, one cannot really talk about a "bare" REF anymore, since we are dealing with two successive independent clauses (PROP and REF), the only link being that the first clause contains a pronominal element which is coreferential with the entire second clause. Nevertheless, such clefts closely resemble those with a subordinate clausal REF discussed above, which justifies treating them as peripheral types of right-dislocation. Such instances clearly show that the RD phenomenon is prototypically organized.

It should be noted, finally, that the REF of these iPSC-RDs need not be clausal; it can also be a simple noun phrase or prepositional phrase expressing a single referent, as in:

(166)   *B: you need sideboards that's what your [be] bedroom*
         lacks . is a [b] is a . [ə:] dressing table on which
         there's a mirror and that's essentially what a side-
         board is (...) (S.4.2.73.3)

Such cases, however, have already been discussed under the more central cases of RD, as they are examples of the core "proposition + referent" pattern.

6.3.6. Summary

In this section, we have attempted to show that the formal category "RD" cannot be strictly delineated according to clear categorial parameters. Rather, what we call RD is a prototypically organized linguistic category consisting of central (cf. parts of section 6.2) and less central (cf. some cases in section 6.2, and all instances in this section) cases.

In the following section, we will be concerned with instances of RD which do not function as repairs. By discussing non-repair RDs, we will try to show that RD is a multifunctional phenomenon.

6.4. Repair-RDs versus non-repair-RDs

6.4.1. Preliminaries

We have already hinted at the existence of RDs which do not function as reflections of an anaphor repair process; in this section, we will offer some empirical evidence towards the claim that RD is a multifunctional phenomenon. Apart from repair, two major functions of RD emerge from our data: its use in the structuring of the information flow in questions (section 6.4.2), and its attitudinal use (section 6.4.3), respectively. We will discuss each of these functions in turn. We will return to this lack of one-to-one correspondence between grammatical form and discourse function in the concluding section of this chapter.

We will also pay attention to the prosody of these non-repair RDs (section 6.5), as it is also relevant to the interactional analysis of our repair data. In chapter 4, we have already dealt at length with some prosodic aspects (pausal behaviour, tone unit structure, and intonation) of self-repairs; in this chapter, we will compare the prosody of repair-RDs to that of non-repair-RDs. Interestingly, there are significant differences between the major functional categories; this means that the prosody of RDs thus indirectly confirms the existence of the different discourse functions of RD.

6.4.2. Repair-related RDs: Question-RDs

In this section, we will look at a sub-class of RDs which have a different function in their own right; however, we will argue that this function is somewhat related to the repair-function discussed in the remainder of this dissertation.

In our data, there are 11 RDs functioning as *yes-no* questions, i.e. as requests for information. We regard the term "question" as a functional label here: we will only regard as questions those utterances which function as genuine requests for information, regardless of their surface form. The term "interrogative", on the other hand, is used as a purely formal label. There are three formal categories of *yes-no* questions:

(167)   Inversion questions; e.g. *Is this a question?*
         Tag questions; e.g. *This is a question, isn't it?*
         Queclaratives; e.g. *This is a question?*

The first two of these have interrogative form; queclaratives, on the other hand, are a combination of declarative form and question-function.

Clearly, not every utterance with interrogative form functions as a real question, i.e. as a request for information or, as is often the case with tag questions and queclaratives, confirmation. As is rightly pointed out by Levinson (1983: 289ff.), there is no principled way of mapping speech acts (e.g. questions) onto utterance types (e.g. interrogatives). In conversation, however, we do have a way of determining the question-status of an utterance, in that genuine questions form the first part of a so-called (question-answer) "adjacency pair" (Sacks—Schegloff—Jefferson 1974). Building on this criterion, in Geluykens (1988c) we have made use of the following recognition procedure for polar questions:

(168)   criterion A: for every turn-final utterance U, assume
             potential question-status;
         criterion B: if U is interrogative, and followed by
             unmarked response, accept question-status; if not,
             look for marked response;
         criterion C: if U is non-interrogative, and followed by
             unmarked response, accept question-status; if not,
             reject U as question.

This procedure, which is based on the assumption that in most cases, form and function will coincide, has a conservative bias, in that any non-interrogative (e.g. a declarative question) with a potential marked response is ruled out of the data.

By an unmarked response we mean, in the case of *yes-no* questions, responses such as confirmation (e.g. *yes*), negation (e.g. *no*), or a statement to the effect that neither confirmation nor negation is possible (e.g. *I don't know*). Sometimes a response is more marked, in the sense that there is no straightforward reply to the question itself, but the preceding utterance is nevertheless clearly interpreted as a question. For instance, instead of answering, the hearer can respond with another question:

(169)   A: *Is this a question?*
         B: *What do you mean?*

Although this is not a typical adjacency pair, the second question is in fact a response to the first one. Marked responses are, of course, relatively rare.

Let us now look at some of our data [without prosodic marking]. We will start with prototypical RDs, i.e. those with an NP as their REF. Later on, we will look at some question-RDs which have a gerund or a sub-clause as their REF. Some of the prototypical RDs are inversion questions:

(170)   B: ((and)) what's the poem about . is it about a cock and
             a fox
         A: that's right in a [he?]
         B: *yes*
         A: *in* a farmyard **((Chaunticleer))**
         B: **is that . is that what** it really is about . a cock
             and a fox
         A: no . not *really (laughs -)*
         B: *((what)) . what is it then*
         A: it's about men and their and it's Chaucer's [∂:] method
             of . by this bare little story - bringing in so many
             other stories to show the folly of men (...)
             (S.3.1.c38.4)

(171)   C: I had to define earthy today . I said John is a very earthy
             person he's only interested in beer and sex . do you
             think that's all right --
         A: Cold Comfort Farm type image
         C: yes that's right exactly so *((6 sylls))*
         A: *have you been listening to that* as well . to [∂:] the
             the Cold Comfort **Farm ((and all that))**
         C: **oh no I** wish I'd known how lovely (S.2.8.b39.5)

There are also a few tag questions, such as instance (172) below; instance (173), on the other hand, does not qualify as a genuine question, as it is not followed by an appropriate resonse:

(172)   B: (...) then that's dropped they have an exam at the end of
             the two terms . and they . then come on ((to)) the full
             honours course . and they have the last term .
             completely . free for revision .
         E: it's given you ((a)) wide range of teaching this course
             hasn't it well over a *period (...)*
         B: *yes I suppose it has*

(173)   [context: on places to practice rock-climbing]
         *B: no training *((several sylls))**
         A: no - mhm -- . <u>it is ridiculous</u> <u>the places you practice on</u>
         <u>isn't it</u> (...)   (S.7.3.f34.9)

There are no prototypical queclarative RDs in our data; there is, however, a non-prototypical one (cf. [181] below).

What is the conversational function of these RDs? From one point of view, their question status in itself of course sets them apart from other RDs; one could leave it at that, and conclude that they are just a special way of asking questions.

However, we would like to go one step further, and ask ourselves why speakers should want to ask a question in the form of a RD, when the majority of questions in conversation of course are not in a RD format. After all, there are non-RD alternatives for all of the data mentioned above; instances (170) and (172), for instance, might just as well have read:

(174)   *Is a cock and a fox what it really is about?*

(175)   *This course has given you a wide range of teaching hasn't it?*

There must be a functional reason which makes speakers use a RD format rather than a non-RD one.

On the one hand, question-RDs are a bit similar, from a semantic point of view, to repair-RDs, in that the REF, as it were, "repairs" the PROP by turning the gap into a semantically more specified form. On the other hand, there are good reasons for regarding them as a functional category in their own right. For one thing, their recoverability status appears to differ somewhat from repair-RDs (cf. infra). Secondly, their prosodic behaviour is different (cf. infra). Most importantly, their behaviour, from an interactional point of view, seems to be different from repair-RDs, in that there is no interactional process with three distinct stages involved, at least not to the same extent as is the case for repair-RDs. In our opinion, question-RDs form a unified whole, in which the speaker does not start off with a PROP and then re-organizes it into a RD, but has a [PROP + REF] organization in mind from the outset. The prosodic and temporal behaviour of question-RDs provides good evidence for this, as we will see below.

In detail, what happens might be the following. The speaker wants to ask a *yes-no* question, in other words he utters a proposition and wants to elicit from the hearer a statement to the effect of whether he (i.e. the hearer) considers the information contained in the proposition true or not.

However, this *yes-no* statement on the part of the hearer could affirm or negate the whole of the *yes-no* question, or any part of it, depending on what part of the question is regarded as presupposed by the hearer (we will not go into the literature on presupposition here; cf. Levinson 1983: chapter 4 for a recent review). For instance, the negation of (176) —assuming that the answer will be negative— could be any of the possibilities in (177), depending on factors such as context, intonation, etc.:

(176)   *Does John love Mary?*

(177)   (a) *No, it is not the case that [John loves Mary].*
         (b) *No, Bill loves Mary.*
         (c) *No, John loves Helen.*
         (d) *No, John hates Mary.*

Answers (177a) to (177d) all have different presuppositional behaviour. Out of these possibilities, it is only (177a) which negates the entire proposition contained in the question; all the other answers negate only part of the proposition, treating the other parts as presupposed. To preserve the parallel with (176), consider now its RD counterpart (178) below:

(178)   *Does he love Mary, John?*

As an answer to (178), unlike for (176), instance (177a) intuitively seems the most appropriate one; (177c) and (177d) are also possible, but (177b) sounds distinctly odd. Indeed, the following exchange is unlikely to occur:

(179)   *A: Does he love Mary, John?*
         B: No, Bill loves Mary.

This implies that, by phrasing a question as a RD rather than as an "ordinary" VS-question, the speaker limits the range of possible answers, in that it becomes impossible to interpret the RD as a question in which the REF itself is the scope of the question. We would argue that this is at least part of the reason why a question-RD format is chosen.

If we have a look at the actual answers to the question-RDs in our data, this claim is not contradicted: in all negative responses (the claim cannot be verified for the positive ones), it is indeed the whole proposition which is being negated rather than the REF by itself. Instance (171) is a good example.

Instance (170) above appears to contradict our claim, in that it is the REF *a cock and a fox* which appears to be the scope of the question. However, due to the context, (170) cannot be considered a typical question-RD. Note that in the first turn of (170), the speaker phrases his question as *what's the poem about . is it about a cock and a fox.* Rather than being a real *yes/no* question, the second part of this is really an addendum to the previous *wh* question, an addendum which limits the range of possible answers. By extension, the rephrasing of the second part in RD format cannot be really considered a genuine *yes-no* question on the same level as the other ones in this section. As it is preceded by a *wh*-question —moreover a *wh*-question which precisely has as its scope the REF (or equivalent referent) of the RD— the presuppositional behaviour of the yes-no-question will be quite different. Instance (170) therefore does not really contradict our claim.

We argue that the REF of the question-RD signals "what the question is about" (we use the term "about" in a non-technical sense here; we do not necessarily wish to imply that the REF is somehow the "topic" of the sentence). Since what the question is about will be to a large extent recoverable (and thus pronominalized by means of the gap), it is hard to imagine it being the sole scope of the negation. However, since the speaker wants to make absolutely sure what the question is about, he does not leave this essential referent pronominal, but specifies it further by means of the REF (despite its recoverability status; we will go into this a bit more deeply below). Using a RD is thus an interactionally sensible thing to do, as it signals more clearly what it is exactly what is being questioned, or rather, what it is that is definitely not being questioned.

The difference between, say, (176) and (178) is quite subtle, and we are not claiming that speakers make a conscious choice about this all the time. However, there is an additional reason why speakers would want to opt for a RD, a reason which is related to the repair argumentation for other RDs, and due to the recoverability status of referents in questions.

If one looks at certain RDs, one notices that, from a purely linear point of view, the REF is not inferable, as is the case for repair-RDs, but rather directly recoverable. In (171), for instance, the REF *Cold Comfort Farm* is explicitly mentioned two turns earlier.

We have already pointed out that the REF represents what the question is "about". Given that the question is pointless without the hearer knowing the precise reference of this, it is very important that the speaker makes it unambiguously clear to the hearer what the precise reference of the gap is. Pronominalization thus works differently in this type of context, due to recoverability being more important in questions, in the sense that it cannot as easily be taken for granted. Once again, this is an argument against a purely informational, linear approach to recoverability.

Let us rephrase this slightly, to make absolutely clear what we mean. In declarative discourse, a speaker may pronominalize something, even though it is only indirectly inferable, and leave the hearer to work out the exact reference. Even if the hearer fails to do so, this does not necessarily mean that interaction will break down (the hearer may find out the reference later on, etc.). In questions, on the other hand, it is crucial that the hearer works out the exact reference straightaway, since he is expected to give an answer to the question in the subsequent turn. Therefore, if there is any doubt whatsoever about the reference of an element in the question (i.e. the gap) —especially if that element is also the presupposed part— it makes sense to add more semantic information on the referent, even in cases where the hearer might normally be expected to work out the reference for himself.

Put differently, this means that the interplay between the E- and the C-principles works differently in questions: it becomes even more vital to be informative enough, even if this is at the expense of economy. Note that this line of reasoning is very much like the repair-explanation offered for non-question RDs, and is in fact quite compatible with it. The only difference would then lie in the fact that a RD format is chosen from the outset in question-RDs, whereas this is not the case in repair-RDs; the prosodics of both categories at least seem to point in that direction (cf. infra).

Having said this, it should be pointed out that some REFs in question-RDs are also inferable rather than directly recoverable. Instance (173) is a case in point, in that the REF *the places you practice on* is indirectly derivable from the entire previous context, and thus inferable. One could argue that these are cases of straighforward repair, were it not for their question-status and their similarity to the other RDs discussed here. It should be clear by now that question-RDs and repair-RDs are functionally closely related.

We have offered two specific functional factors which contribute towards the use of a question-RD. Firstly, there is a semantic difference between a question-RD and an ordinary VS-question, in that their expectancies regarding the scope of the answer are slightly different. Secondly, there is an interactional difference, in that recoverability of the gap is more crucial in questions than it is in other discourse contexts. These two factors are compatible, and probably combine in most cases. In some ways, therefore, question-RDs are like repair-RDs, in that the REF amplifies a referring expression that may not be clear, in the sense that it may not be sufficiently recoverable in the circumstances. In other ways, question-RDs are unlike repair-RDs, in that they lack the collaborative dimension of repair-RDs. We will see further on that their prosody is unlike both repair-RDs and emotive RDs, which seems to confirm their distinct functional status.

Before we go into emotive RDs, let us look briefly at a small subset of question-RDs. Just as is the case with repair-RDs, there are instances in which the REF is not a simple referent, expressed by an NP (or PP), but rather an entire proposition in its own right, expressed by a gerundial clause or subordinate clause. As we have already discussed the prototypical organization of RD in some detail elsewhere, it will suffice here to give some examples from our database.

First of all, there are three instances of a gerundial REF, e.g. (180) and (181) below:

(180)   A: *isn't this going to be a strange and impossible task for me picking up linguistics and I'm entirely at least almost entirely ignorant of it at present . (S.1.5.1.1)*

(181)   A: *I don't think they really have anything new to say - [∂] I*
              read one book . [∂] - well we'll leave which one it was
         B: *mhm*
         A: *and . really it didn't tell me anything new . at all ((as a))*
              matter of fact it was rather boring .
         B: <u>*you don't think it helps*</u> *((from [?])) .* <u>*judging a book*</u>
              <u>*from its stylistic point of view*</u> *.*
         A: *[∂:m] . to an extent I I I I find . [∂:m] --*
         B: *in the structure -*
         A: *to an extent not a lot (S.5.9.96.5)*

Instance (181) is a queclarative (the only one in the data), i.e. an
utterance with declarative form functioning as a question. There are
also three instances of a clausal REF; an example:

(182)   A: *I mean she can't stand you know being being more than -*
              two and a half inches off . (([thi:])) ground anyway ---
         B: <u>*is this right for everybody*</u> *what* **I'm* . doing*
         C: **mhm* that's fine --- (S.1.11.a32.8)*

Functionally, these RDs are all similar to the prototypical ones
discussed in the previous section, so we need not discuss them in
detail.

6.4.2. Non-repair-related RDs: Emotive RDs

In this section, we will discuss RDs which do not function as repairs
and which, moreover, have a function which is totally unrelated to
repair. We will label these Emotive RDs, for reasons which will
become clear later on.
     Let us start off by looking at some data; these RDs all have in
common that the REF is a pronominal form rather than a full lexical
NP:

(183)   B: *yes quite - . well if you will ask leading questions *--**
         A: **(-- laughs)* . yes* <u>*that was a bit of a swine that*</u> *- .*

(184)   B: *(...) -* <u>*it was -- oh a real shambles ((that)).*</u> *when*
              I think back . (...) (S.1.12.29.5)

(185)   *A: (...) - [ə:m] . well I mean it's a . terribly difficult*
         question to answer that because . it entirely depends
         on the person . (S.2.2.a75.4)

(186)   *A: that's very frightening that .*
         B: (...) (S.2.4.a48.5)

These RDs have one thing in common, viz. the fact that, from the point of view of referential disambiguation, the REF is superfluous. Since the REF does not add significantly to the semantic specification of the gap, and is in fact semantically equally non-specific, these RDs cannot be treated in terms of repair. Also, since the REF is directly recoverable from the context (and thus easy to keep pronominalized; e.g. [183]), they lack the feature of problematic recoverability present in repair-RDs.

What, then, makes speakers decide to opt for a RD format? After all, given the fact that two pronominal forms are used (the gap and the REF) to refer to one and the same recoverable referent, this looks like a violation of the Economy principle without any interference from the Clarity principle.

We think the explanation must be sought on another level altogether, viz. on the attitudinal one. Indeed, on closer inspection, it appears that in all these RDs, a common factor is the fact that the speaker has either a positive or a negative attitude towards the gap/REF-referent. RDs, then, might be a way of expressing negative or positive speaker-connotation with regard to a referent; this is why we have chosen the label emotive RD for these instances. In the majority of cases, the speaker attitude seems to be negative; instances (183) to (186) above are cases in point. In some cases, however —e.g. (189) and (191) below—, the attitudinal overtone is clearly positive, so it would be a mistake to regularly associate emotive RDs with negative speaker attitudes.

This function of RD is obviously very different from the ones discussed earlier. Whereas for question-RDs, there is a slight similarity with repair-RDs, in that the REF is sometimes inferable, this is not the case for emotive RDs. It may be that it is only by virtue of the REF being very much recoverable, and thus in no need of repair from a referential point of view, that speakers can exploit RDs in this fashion.

This would mean that the emotive use of RD is to some extent parasitic on the repair function, in the sense that, by virtue of using a RD, and thus violating the E-principle, the speaker signals that there is some additional dimension of meaning to his utterance. In ordinary circumstances, the hearer would interpret this in referential terms, i.e. would assume that the speaker uses a RD in order to repair an unfelicitous referential form. The fact that such an explanation is blatantly impossible in these cases may then lead the hearer to try an alternative explanation. To put it in Gricean terms, by pretending to be to some extent unco-operative (i.e. violating the E-principle) the speaker creates an intended implicature on the part of the hearer, viz. to look for an aspect of meaning, apart from the referential level, in which the RD might be more informational than a non-RD format would have been. The attitudinal level is an obvious candidate; the RD can then be interpreted as a token for the signalling of the speaker's inner thoughts. The speaker thus exploits the typical repair-function of RDs to signal another meaning aspect. In other words, emotive RDs only look as if they violate the E-principle; in practice, the less economical RD format is indeed due to some kind of C-principle, albeit that "clarity" has to be understood here not in terms of referential information, but in terms of attitudinal factors.

Note that this emotive use of linguistic forms is not restricted to RD. It has been observed (Barbara Fox, personal communication) that speakers in other circumstances sometimes use full NPs rather than pronominal forms in order to mark a —usually negative— attitude towards a referent. An example would be *that guy was really too much* in a context where a simple *he* would have sufficed from a referential point of view. Such instances can also be explained in terms of the apparent flouting of the E-principle to create an implicature; our two pragmatic principles can thus be shown to have more general applicability and explanatory value.

In the above instances, the REF is a simple pronoun, but there are also cases in which the REF is a, semantically equally empty, lexical NP:

(187)   *A: there's a chap there he's got a degree that fellow - .*
         old Joe (...) (S.1.7.125.4)

(188)   *B: (...) - ((I mean it's)) absolutely pathetic that sort of*
         thing darling even I don't do that (S.2.10.51.3)

(189)   B: (...) I thought *it was jolly funny the whole thing* and
              rather a sophisticated sense of humour ((presumably))
              --- darling (...) (S.2.10.71.7)

(190)   A: (...) and *he's a real . vicious swine that number* -- .
              but he bought Sabre -- with all his savings --
              (S.2.13.135.6)

(191)   B: (...) she's been talking about leaving and going to a
              train . teacher's training college --
          A: ((but)) *she's brilliant that girl*
          B: I know . well (...) (S.6.2.81.3)

In all these cases, the REF contains a semantically general noun
(*thing*, etc.) which is, from an referential point of view, almost
totally superfluous. The RD thus merely creates an attitudinal
connotation.

There are a few RDs which on the face of it look like emotive
ones, but which may actually be repair-related, in that the REF might
refer to gestural deixis. In a way, the REF would thus be referentially
more informative than the gap, although at first sight it appears to be
as semantically empty as the REFs mentioned above. This line of
reasoning might apply to the following instances in the data, which
all come from the same context, in which the participants are looking
at a series of paintings (which are thus all indirectly recoverable, but
prone to being confused):

(192)   A: mhm - yes I like that one in the corner but I don't really
              want a portrait in my room I like . my own .
          B: *yes yes . yes .* mhm
          A: *individuality to spread around the room* - . *it's nice that*
              --- yes it is so Brenda this is (...) (S.1.8.9.6)

(193)   A: *you* say this is . who is this Velasquez
          B: [ə] *it's a copy of a Velasquez that* and I don't . [əsh]
              copies are not such fun (...) (S.1.4.39.4)

(194)   B: *that* big one or . yes this looks better when you can't
              see it too far *it's not so good when you can see it*
              sharply this one --- (S.1.4.51.8)

The problem is that it is difficult to interpret these unambiguously. The very nature of our database —non-videotaped material— makes it impossible to find out for sure whether there is really gestural deixis involved. If so, these RDs are repair-related, in that the gap, which might be referentially unclear by virtue of interference from the other extralinguistically recoverable referents, is "repaired" by means of a pronominal (deictic) REF accompanied by kinetic, gestural information. This would thus show that recoverability can also be influenced by extralinguistic factors, as pointed out in chapter 5. This analysis in terms of deixis, plausible as it may sound, must remain tentative for lack of conclusive evidence; strictly speaking, these RDs might also be emotive.

To finish this discussion of non-repair RDs, let us have a look at one example in our database which is a non-prototypical RD as well as being a non-repair one:

(195)   A: *for example that [ə:m] -- [ə] the Mill Bank . *Tower**
         b: *I was thinking* of that one
         A: yeah . **yeah**
         b: **at that** moment -
         A: in a slightly mist down below *and* [ə]
         b: *mhm* -- <u>one of my favourite modern buildings that</u>
         A: yeah --- (S.4.4.47.5)

This RD is non-prototypical from a syntactic point of view, as there is no overt gap. It is , however, easy to imagine the PROP to be elliptical for *it is one of my favourite modern buildings* , so one is justified in regarding this as an instance of RD, albeit a more preipheral one from a formal point of view.

6.5. Prosodic aspects of repair- versus non-repair-RDs

6.5.1. Preliminaries

In this section, we will look at three prosodic aspects of question-RDs and emotive RDs, and compare them to repair-RDs: the occurrence of pauses and turns after the PROP (Table 7), the occurrence of tone unit boundaries in the same location (Table 8), and the intonation at the end of the PROP (Table 9).

Table 7. Number of pauses+turns in emotive, question and repair RDs

	emotive	question	repair
[+turn]	— (0.0%)	— (0%)	15 (16%)
[+pause]	1 (6%)	5 (45%)	44 (46%)
[-turn/pause]	17 (94%)	6 (55%)	37 (38%)
total	18 (100%)	11 (100%)	96 (100%)

Table 8. Tone unit boundary between PROP and REF in RDs

	emotive	question	repair
# PROP + REF #	16 (94%)	1 (17%)	— (0%)
# PROP # REF #	1 (6%)	5 (83%)	37 (100%)
Total	17	6	100

Table 9. Intonation of PROP in emotive, question and repair RDs

	emotive	question	repair
fall	17	4	61
rise-fall	—	1	9
rise	1	4	4
fall-rise	—	1	10
fall+rise	—	1	11
falling	17 (94%)	5 (45%)	70 (74%)
rising	1 (6%)	6 (55%)	25 (26%)
total	18	11	95

6.5.2. The prosody of question-RDs

In this section, we will discuss the prosodic behaviour of question-RDs; we will attempt to show that they differ from both repair-RDs and non-repair-RDs in several respects. In doing so, we will provide indirect evidence for our functional analysis.

Table 7 represents the occurrence of pauses and/or turns in question-RDs as opposed to repair-RDs and emotive RDs. It can be observed that question-RDs differ significantly from both other types, as far as their pausal behaviour is concerned. Whereas repair-RDs mostly have a pause (or even a turn) inbetween PROP and REF, and emotive RDs almost never have such a pause, question-RDs are situated inbetween these two extremes. There is thus evidence for regarding them as a functional category in their own right. On the one hand, the occasional occurrence of pauses (albeit in only 45% of the cases) suggests that they are less far removed functionally from repair-RDs than are emotive RDs. On the other hand, pauses are significantly less frequent than they are in repair-RDs, which suggests that question-RDs indeed lack the three-move interactional dimension of repair-RDs. Indirectly, these figures also confirm the interactional account given for the occurrence of pauses as initiations of the repair in repairs-RDs (chapter 4).

Let us now turn our attention towards the occurrence of a tone unit boundary between PROP and REF (table 8). Naturally, those RDs which have a pause/turn inbetween the PROP and the REF almost always have a tone unit boundary inbetween these two parts; table 2 therefore only deals with RDs without an intervening pause/turn. Just as is the case for repair-RDs, question-RDs nearly always have a tone unit boundary between PROP and REF. Even in the one instance where this is not the case, there is a kind of boundary present:

(196)   B: #/is this 'right for 'everybody [/what I'm . 'doing #]#

The REF here in fact does have its own tone unit, the only difference with the other ones being that it is a subordinate one (cf. Crystal 1969: 244-247 for his theory of subordination of tone units). The absence of an "ordinary" tone unit boundary thus does not mean that the REF does not have its own nucleus. In fact, if one treats subordinate tone units as tone units in their own right, as we will do here (most other prominent British models of intonation, such as O'Connor and Arnold 1961, Halliday 1968, Brazil 1975, and Cruttenden 1986, do not allow for the existence of such tone units; cf. also Gussenhoven 1984), it follows that all REFs in question-RDs have an independent tone unit.

We can conclude that, as far as tonality is concerned, question-RDs differ significantly from emotive RDs, which in most cases do not have a tone unit boundary between PROP and REF, and are comparable to repair-RDs. This in fact fits in quite well with what one would expect, given the fact that in both repair-RDs and question-RDs, the "information value" of the REF is quite high. In question-RDs, since the REF signals "what the question is about", and since its exact reference must be made very clear, is is quite important that it is given some form of prosodic prominence, to facilitate comprehension for the hearer.

We can now turn to the intonation of RDs, more specifically to the final pitch movement of the PROP. As was the case with repair-RDs, this is the most important tone from a functional point of view, as it marks the boundary between the two major parts of the RD. Figures are represented in Table 9.

Interestingly, the PROP in question-RDs, unlike that in repair-RDs and emotive RDs, is more likely to end in a rising tone (55%) than in a falling tone (45%); this increase in rising tones turns out to be significant. This observation supports the claim that, although the function of question-RDs can be considered to be somewhat related to rapair-RDs, they should definitely not be treated as being functionally identical.

The reason why speakers feel more inclined to use a rising tone to end the PROP in question-RDs must probably be sought in their different interactional behaviour. Unlike repair-RDs, for which one must talk in terms of two separate stages in an interactional process, the PROP and REF of question-RDs belong together more closely, and form an interactional whole; this also shows in the lower frequency of pauses between PROP and REF.

Both the pausal and intonational behaviour of question-RDs seem to suggest that they form a communicative whole. The speaker does not repair his utterance, but organizes it, from the outset, in such a way that it is communicatively more efficient, in that what the question is "about" is set off from the rest of the proposition, and is repeated in a semantically more specified way. We have already gone into this at length in the preceding section, so we need not repeat this line of reasoning here.

The rising tone at the end of the PROP, then, is an incompleteness cue, both from a syntactic and interactional point of view. From a syntactic point of view, it marks the sentence as being incomplete, in the sense that further specification is to follow. More importantly, from an interactional point of view, the rising tone is a turn-holding cue, signalling to the hearer that the speaker's contribution is not yet finished. The function of intonation as a non-finality or incompleteness marker is well attested in the literature (cf. Bolinger 1982, 1986; Cruttenden 1981, 1986; Geluykens 1988c).

6.5.3. The prosody of emotive RDs

In much the same way as we did for question-RDs, we will look at three different aspects of emotive RDs: tonality and tonicity, the occurrence of pauses or turns, and the intonation of the PROP-part of the RD.

First of all, let us consider the occurrence of pauses inbetween PROP and REF. Table 7 gives the figures for emotive RDs compared to repair-RDs and question-RDs. In this respect, the prosody of emotive RDs obviously differs significantly from both repair-RDs and emotive RDs. There is only one emotive RD with a pause, viz. (197):

(197)   C: *ah but* <u>that is part of the - . the Lord Thompson</u>
              isn't it . <u>that one</u> . **((syll))**
         a: **ah** well it may be
         C: (...) (S.2.7.112.2)

Note that this is also a question-RD, so the pause might be due to the RDs question status. In none of the other emotive RDs is there a pause after the PROP; this suggests that, from an interactional point of view, emotive RDs can be considered to be one single utterance rather than a combination of different stages (as is the case in repair-RDs). Their pausal behaviour thus indirectly confirms that emotive RDs are a separate functional category.

Secondly, we will have a look at the occurrence of tone unit boundaries inbetween the PROP and the REF (tonality), and at the possible occurrence of a tonic nucleus on the REF (tonicity). Table 8 represents the tonality of emotive RDs, as opposed to repair-RDs and question-RDs. One will recall that one emotive RD has a pause inbetween PROP and REF, and is excluded from the figures below; the total number of emotive RDs is thus 17.

These figures show that, on top of not having a pause, emotive RDs also do not have a prosodic boundary of another kind between their two respective parts. Needless to say, this differs significantly from the situation in both question- and repair-RDs. There is only one RD in which the REF has a separate tone unit, and even this is a somewhat special case:

(198)   B: [ə] *it's a "/`copy # of a Vel`lasquez [/`that #]* #
         (S.1.4.39.4)

In this instance, the REF consists of a subordinate tone unit. However, since we have argued in our discussion of question-RDs that we will regard such tone units as independent tone units in their own right, we will assume there to be a tone unit boundary after the PROP here. Note, however, that the status of (198) as an emotive RD is uncertain (cf. our discussion in section 6.4.2), in that it might be an instance of gestural deixis.

The fact that, in the vast majority of cases, there is no tone unit boundary between PROP and REF should not be taken to mean that the REF never has a nuclear accent. Indeed, there are a few instance where the RD carries a compound tone, i.c. a [fall+rise], the second nucleus of which falls on the REF-part of the RD; e.g.:

(199)   A: (...) - . *it's `nice ´that* # --- *(S.1.8.9.6)*

In most cases, though, the REF does not have a separate nuclear accent.

In other words, unlike repair- and question-RDs, emotive RDs mostly have neither a tone unit boundary between PROP and REF nor a tonic nucleus on their REF. This is hardly surpriring, given the fact that in emotive RDs the REF is unimportant, from a referential point of view. There is thus no reason for the speaker to highlight it by means of tonality or tonicity.

Finally, let us consider the intonation of emotive RDs, more particularly the final tone of the PROP. Figures are represented in table 9. It is clear from these figures that the PROP of emotive RDs mostly ends in a falling pitch movement; this differs significantly from question-RDs (but not from repair-RDs). The fact that the tone on the PROP is, in most cases, also the final tone of the RD (the REF having no separate nucleus) probably means that other factors, such as turn taking after the entire RD, attitudinal elements, etc. influence the choice of either a fall or a rise. At any rate, the fall on the PROP, unlike in repair-RDs, where it is usually accompanied by a pause, should not be taken to be a floor-yielding cue.

6.5.4. Summary of prosodic analysis

Summing up the prosodic situation in the three main functional types of RD, we can conclude that there are significant differences between all three functional categories. The situation is as follows:

(200)   repair: pause/turn between PROP and REF
                        REF has separate tone unit
                        falling tone on PROP;
         question: mostly no intervening pause/turn
                        REF has separate tone unit
                        rising tone on PROP;
         emotive: no intervening pause/turn
                        PROP and REF form one tone unit
                        falling tone on PROP.

The prosodic behaviour of RDs thus offers further, independent evidence in favour of our functional analysis.

6.6. Conclusion

In this chapter, we have attempted to show several things. First of all, it was argued that the syntactic category "RD" is, in a lot of cases, the direct reflection of an interactional process, i.c. the process whereby the speaker himself repairs an informationally inadequate anaphoric form. In other words, grammatical form is a reflection of communicative function.

It was also argued that the formal category RD is prototypically organized (cf. Lakoff 1987), and defies strict delineation for several reasons. The decision what and what not to regard as a RD thus to some extent arbitrary, due to the category having fuzzy edges. We will return to this in more detail in chapter 10.

Thirdly, and finally, it was shown that RD is a multifunctional phenomenon, and that there is no one-to-one correspondence between grammatical form and discourse function. Apart from repair, two other major functions of RD were discussed: its use in yes-no questions, and its use for attitudinal reasons. In later chapters, we will show that this lack of one-to-one correspondence between form and function also works the other way around: not only is it the case that not all RDs function as repairs, it is also the case that not all repairs surface as RDs. We thus get a fairly complex situation in which form (RD) and function (repair) only partially overlap.

Chapter 7

Other-initiated other-repairs

7.1. Introduction: On the relevance of other-repairs

In our analysis of self-repair and (chapters 3 to 5), we have argued RD to be an instantiation of either other-initiated self-repair, or self-initiated self-repair. If this claim is indeed correct (and we have already provided much evidence for its correctness), one would expect there to be instances in which the reparandum and reparans are not uttered by the same speaker (as in RD), but in which the reparans (the REF) is uttered by another participant. In other words, given the fact that there are (at least) four interactional types of repair, our claim about the repair function of RD would be strengthened considerably if related instances of *other* -repair were to be found, in which PROP and REF are uttered by different speakers.

We have also claimed the pragmatic principles outlined in chapter 2 to have general applicability, and have argued that the anaphor repairs discussed in this study provide strong empirical evidence for the tension existing between Clarity and Economy. For that reason as well, other-repairs could provide important evidence both for the generality of the pragmatic principles and for the claim that anaphor repairs reflect the tension between them.

In this section, we will show that such other-repairs indeed occur, and that they are indeed functionally very similar to the self-repairs labelled "RD". The term RD, then, becomes nothing more or less than a label, a cover-term for those informativeness-repairs which are self-correcting (and which have a "bare" reparans; as we will see in the next chapters, there are some types of anaphor repairs which cannot be related to RD). The other-repairs discussed in this section thus form strong independent evidence in favour of our functional analysis in the previous chapters.

The fact that other-correcting informativeness repairs are relatively rare (there are only 14 instances in our data) is not that surprising, given the natural preference for self- over other-repair noted in the literature. It should also be pointed out that we have not come across any *self*-initiated, other-correcting repairs in our corpus (a few such cases are discussed elsewhere, however). This is in fact to be more or less expected, given the way the repair mechanism is organized. There is a natural tendency for self- over other-correction in conversation anyway, but whenever the speaker himself initiates a repair, this tendency is even more outspoken, the simple reason being that, since the speaker himself has signalled an inappropriateness, he will also be most likely to know how it can be repaired. Moreover, the initiation of the repair in itself serves as a floor-holding cue. All this explains the virtual absence of self-initiated other-repairs in this study. The discussion which follows will thus be concerned exclusively with other-initiated, other-correcting repairs.

In section 7.2, we will first discuss how the other-repair process operates from an interactional point of view. In section 7.3, we will analyze the repairs from the point of view of information flow.

7.2. Interactional analysis

7.2.1. Prototypical patterning of other-repairs

Let us start off by examining a relatively clear example of other-initiated other-repair in some detail:

(201)   A: *and old Joe who's very [ə:m] . sceptical about these*
            things he's [ə:m] --- you know # he's he was /quite
            /`very im'pressed with *'this this /`'Guinness #
        a: **Joe . Joe Lemon m**
        A: */Joe `Lemon # /^yeah # .* (...) (S.1.7.50.6)*

The reparandum *he* in the first turn is repaired in the hearer-turn by means of the bare NP *Joe Lemon;* we thus get a structure which resembles a RD sequence, the only difference being the fact that the two parts are uttered by different participants. The decision whether to call this a RD or not is in fact a bit arbitrary, in that one could equally well argue such peripheral cases still to be RDs; this once again proves the point that this linguistic category has fuzzy edges, as we have argued before. We will in fact employ the REF-gap terminology occasionally to refer to reparans and reparandum, respectively.

We have to take note of an important interactional feature in (201), viz. the fact that the reparans, after it is uttered by the hearer, is confirmed by the speaker (cf. *Joe Lemon yeah* in the third turn). We argue here that such acknowledgment is a vital ingredient in other-repairs. Indeed, the hearer can at most make an educated guess about the reference of the pronominal gap (only the speaker, of course, knowing the referent), and not be entirely sure about it (otherwise, a repair would not be necessary in the first place!), It is thus essential that this tentatively offered information is acknowledged, and reference thus, collaboratively and unambiguously, established. The interactional process taking place can be summed up in the following way:

(202)   step 1 (speaker): PROP with reparandum (gap)
          step 2 (hearer):   a) initiation of repair
                              b) correction through reparans (REF)
          step 3 (speaker): acknowledgment of reparans

This third step, we thus claim, is an essential step in the interactional other-repair process. The remainder of our data appears to confirm this (so do the few instances of self-initiated other-repair in our data, incidentally, as we will see in chapter 8). Of course, the attempt at repair on the part of the hearer can be wrong, in which case we do not get confirmation from the speaker, but rejection, probably implicitly, by providing the correct reparans; e.g.:

(203)   A: *he was quite impressed with this Guinness*
          B: *Joe Lemon*
          A: *Joe Wright I mean (constructed).*

The result is then, in effect, an other-initiated, *self* -correcting repair (with an other-correcting attempt), which in most cases qualifies as a kind of RD (we have indeed come across a few such cases in chapter 3). Once again, we see that the borderline between other-initiated other-repairs repairs and RD-repairs is very vague indeed.

Another thing which ought to be pointed out in (201) is the fact that the reparandum, as in RDs, has a problematic recoverability status, which leads to a clash between the E- and C-principles. More specifically, the referent is inferable, in that it is partially recoverable (cf. *Joe* earlier on in the first turn), but not entirely so; it is clear that some inferential work is still needed, due to the fact that *Joe* in itself can refer to more than one referent. The reparans *Joe Lemon* resolves this ambiguity. The recoverability status of the reparandum thus also shows the close resemblance between the repairs discussed here and the ones labelled "RD". We will return to this in section 7.3. The important thing to remember here is that these repairs, too, appear to point towards a clash between, on the one hand, Economy (and hence the use of a pronominal form in the first instance), and, on the other hand Clarity (and hence the necessary repairing of that pronominal by means of a full NP).

There are several other, comparable instances of this prototypical repair exchange in the data; let us just consider a few, without going into detail. The following is a small selection:

(204)   *B: what's the latest news on all that*
        A: ooh well . apparently Trumpington . which I applied to
            have not written for references yet which doesn't
            bode very well - . but [ə] -- . they seem to be so
            inefficient anyway - .
        B: they're in the middle of exams --- ((I mean mightn't that
            be the explanation))
        A: yes # --- it would be "/very 'much a second `choice
            [/`anyway #] #
        C: /`what # /^Trumpington # --
        B: ((well yes)) it's so ((awful)) (S.4.6.a38.8)

The following instance has an iPSC-type PROP (compare the non-prototype RDs with such a PROP in chapter 6) (Note that this is partially a NS instance in a surreptitious file, so there is no prosodic marking):

(205)   *A: oh maps must have existed certainly - (coughs) oh the*
            French would have mapped it very - carefully yes --
            well I mean this bears the mark of being a kind of
            independent survey doesn't it
        a: I know that's what's curious
        B: what you /mean the `English . [/àspect 'of it #] # ---

I believe it's a bit of an amalgam ((this map))
(S.2.3.8.5)

The following instance is also interesting, in that it has a non-prototypical REF, viz. a complete sub-clause rather than a NP; it thus also resembles the non-prototypical cases of RD which we discussed in chapter 6:

(206)   B: *I think really that the people speak most of the speakers .*
             were very well known names in this . field and it's
             interesting to go and cast an eye on them really # .
             ((I mean)) I /think 'that's *the `´main thing #*
         A: **((to /see))* the state of the `art ´really # (...)*
             (S.2.8.b17.1)

In instance (207), finally, initiation occurs only after some delay:

(207)   B: *(...) I can't find anything that I could say is Russian (...)*
         d: *(one long turn intervening)*
         B: *well [∂:m] . I mean that is . the most obvious [∂n] [∂:]*
             example but [∂: ? ∂] if they talk about unemployment .
         d: *m*
         B: */they'll ¯say # the /unem¯ployed # /they should be 'made*
             to 'do some . some `work # and /not . scrounge 'off
             the `´state #
         d: *m*
         B: *[∂:m]*
         d: *what [?] . sorry Russians*
         B: *m (S.2.11.b48.7)*

In all these instances, we get a referential process of the type outlined in (202) above.

7.2.2. *Yes-No* questions

No less than 6 out of 14 instances of other-initiated other-repair occur in utterances functioning as *yes-no* questions; these thus deserve some special attention. First, consider a few examples:

(208)   *A: I wish I'd known I'd be coming here this week I would*
            *have got two tickets and we could have gone *you*
            *see**
        *b: *m* .*
        A: m - or even three # /do you like things like 'that # -
        c: like Cosi Fan Tutteyes
        A: oh yes (...) (S.1.10.125.3)

(209)   *a: (...) *when did Eliot stop writing poetry* .*
        A: [ə:m] -- oh the last one was Four Quartets - **[əm]***
        *B: **you** /don't think there's 'any 'poetry in the `drama*
            [/since`then #] # -
        A: /[sn] /since 'Murder In The Cath^edral # [ə:]
        B: m yes . (S.3.5.a3.4)

(210)   *B: ((5-6 sylls)) laundry but it's got a freezer in it**
        *A: we're gonna have an **extension ((3-4 sylls))***
        *D: **but when our extension** is done . we shall have*
            *space at the side and we shall *probably**
        *C: *they /ought* to be out^side # /^anyway # /^oughtn't*
            they #
        B: /`m #
        D: /`what # the /`'freezer #
        C: the /'freezer # (...) (S.4.3.23.1)

These are instances of an inversion question, a queclarative, and a tag
question, respectively; in other words, all three formal types of *yes-
no* question are represented in the database.

   Naturally, these questions are a bit reminiscent of the question-
RDs discussed in chapter 6. The difference is, however, that,
whereas the RDs in chapter 6 are not (or not exclusively) real repairs,
the other-initiation and other-correction in the instances mentioned
here leaves no doubt about their true repair status.

   Nevertheless, there is an important parallel here, viz. the fact that
in questions, the informational status of the gap may become even
more crucial than in other utterances. Put differently: in order to
answer a *yes-no* question, it is vital that the hearer unambiguously
identifies the referents being mentioned in the question. There is thus
a subtle shift in the functioning of the E- and C-principles, in that
being sufficiently informative becomes very important. If the hearer

is in the least doubtful, he may thus initiate a repair. This explains why, even in cases where the reparandum is fairly easily recoverable, like *the freezer* in (210), the hearer may still feel the need to make sure. Having said this, the recoverability status of the reparandum may be comparable to other repairs, in that there is a clear clash between E- and I-principle. In (209), for instance, the REF *Cosi fan Tutti* is both distant and has interference from a few other referents; in (210), the REF *since Murder in the Cathedral* is only indirectly inferable from the context.

We will finish this discussion by mentioning a repair in a question which has a non-prototype reparans:

(211)   B: *how many times is . Hamlet alone with his mother . as*
                  he is in the closet --- ((can you remember))
           A: *[ðm] --- I think it's just that one *scene**
           B: **just* that one scene yes ((and isn't that)) perhaps the*
                  reason why the ghost appears in that scene .
           A: *mhm perhaps yeah*
           B: */well can you see what 'point . there 'may be in 'that # - .*
           A: *in /just ap'pearing in the one ^scene #*
           B: *when Hamlet is alone with his mother (S.3.5.a48.2)*

The REF here is a kind of gerundial clause, and thus resembles the non-prototypical RDs mentioned in chapter 6. Note, incidentally, that the REF *just appearing in the one scene* is indirectly inferable from the immediately preceding context (cf. the following section).

Summing up this section, we can say that the instances of other-initiated other-repair discussed here fit in quite well with the cases of RD-repair analyzed in chapters 3 to 5. As such, they provide strong supporting evidence in favour of our claim that RD is an instantiation of informativeness-repair. Our analysis also shows that the same tension between Economy and Clarity is responsible for the other-repairs in our data.

7.3. Information flow and other-repairs

In this section, we will attempt to show that the other-initiated other-repairs discussed in this chapter are generated by recoverability problems similar to the ones we have already mentioned for self-repairs in previous chapters. It is this problematic status of the reparandum with regard to the preceding discourse context which gives rise to the clash between the Clarity and the Economy principle. The three factors influencing a referent's informational status, i.c. inferability, referential distance, and interference, once again show up here; we will discuss each of them in turn.

7.3.1. Inferability

As was the case with self-repairs, a number of anaphor repairs are generated by the fact that the reparandum is not recoverable directly from the preceding context, but is only retrievable in an indirect way, through inferential linking. Instance (212) below is a good example of this:

(212)   B: how many times is . Hamlet alone with his mother . as he
          is in the closet --- ((can you remember))
          A: [∂m] --- I think it's just that one *scene*
          B: *just* that one scene yes ((and isn't that)) perhaps the
          reason why the ghost appears in that scene .
          A: mhm perhaps yeah
          B: well can you see what point . there may be in that - .
          A: in just appearing in the one scene
          B: when Hamlet is alone with his mother (S.3.5.a48.2)

In this instance, the reparans *just appearing in the one scene* is indirectly derivable from the first two turns of the exchange. It is not mentioned explicitly anywhere in the preceding context, so there is no real explicit antecedent. By over-estimating this referent's recoverability status, the speaker has thus violated the Clarity principle, which gives rise to the hearer-initiated hearer-repair.

Another instance of inferability, this time of a slightly different nature, is (213) below:

(213)   A: and old Joe who's very [∂:m] . sceptical about these
          things he's [∂:m] --- you know # he's he was /quite
          /`very im'pressed with *`this this /`´Guinness #
          a: *Joe . Joe Lemon m*
          A: /Joe `Lemon # /^yeah # .* (...) (S.1.7.50.6)

Part of the reparans *Joe Lemon* in (213) is in fact directly recoverable from the preceding context. However, this antecedent is not enough to allow the hearer to correctly identify the intended referent.

A third and final example of inferability, this time through a scenario-type semantic link, is (214):

(214)   *a: (...) *when did Eliot stop writing poetry* .*
    A: [∂:m] -- oh the last one was Four Quartets - **[∂m]***
    *B: **you** /don't think there's 'any 'poetry in the `drama*
        [/since`then #] # -
    A: /[sn] /since 'Murder In The Cath^edral # [∂:]
    B: m yes . (S.3.5.a3.4)

The whole of this conversation has been concerned with *Eliot;* the reparans *Murder in the Cathedral* is obviously part of this *Eliot* -scenario, but has not been mentioned explicitly in the immediately preceding context. Once again, this results in problematic recoverability, which gives rise to the repair.

7.3.2. Referential Distance

There are a few cases in our data where recoverability becomes problematic, despite the fact that the antecedent of the reparandum has been mentioned in the preceding context. What is involved in these cases is that there is a large amount of referential distance between mention of the antecedent and mention of the to-be-repaired pronoun, which means that recoverability of reference can no longer be taken for granted. Instance (215) is a good example of this:

(215)   *A: (...) I think it's tomorrow is Cosi fan Tutte .*
    b: oh good - nice mixture .
    *A: well it's just as it came you *see**
    *b: *fine* . it's very good .*
    A: and I'm going to see [∂:m] . Borkmann one [∂]
        *Happy Happy Days which I'm **quite looking*
        *forward have***
    *b: **m . lovely***
    A: you seen that

> *b: no . m .*
> *A: I wish I'd known I'd be coming here this week I would*
> *   have got two tickets and we could have gone *you*
> *   see**
> *b: *m* .*
> *A: m - or even three do you like things <u>like that</u> -*
> *c: <u>like Cosi Fan Tutte</u> yes*
> *A: oh yes (...) (S.1.10.125.3)*

The antecedent of the reparandum *that* in speaker A's turn is *Cosi Fan Tutte,* which is last mentioned in the first turn of the exchange. This long distance apparently leads to its recoverability having eroded, as it gives rise to the other-repair in the next to last turn. Note, moreover, that there is another candidate for coreference in the preceding context (*Happy Days*), which means that there is also some degree of interference (cf. the following section) from another referent.

Instance (216) below exhibits a combination of inferability and referential distance:

(216)   *B: (...) I can't find anything that I could say is Russian (...)*
> *d: (one long turn intervening)*
> *B: well [∂:m] . I mean that is . the most obvious [∂n] [∂:]*
> *   example but [∂: ? ∂] if they talk about unemployment .*
> *d: m*
> *B: /they'll ‾say # the /unem‾ployed # /they should be 'made*
> *   to 'do some . some ˋwork # and /not . scrounge 'off*
> *   the ˋˊstate #*
> *d: m*
> *B: [∂:m]*
> *d: what [?] . sorry <u>Russians</u>*
> *B: m (S.2.11.b48.7)*

This instance features a combination of inferability and distance. First of all, the reparans *Russians* is not mentioned explicitly in the preceding context, but is only inferable indirectly through the mention of *Russian* in the first turn. Secondly, mention of this antecedent is quite some distance removed from its being uttered in pronominalized form as the reparandum.

Instance (217) below, finally, is a very interesting example of referential distance, due to the nature of the intervening material:

(217)   A: (...) he won the men's doubles last year didn't he .
         B: oh . and he's got it (. laughs)
         A: and he's got . you know another one as well
         B: . oh I see -
         A: and we need . need them tonight so we can give them
              back . to somebody else
         B: (- laughs) yes yes this is a problem
         A: this is indeed the truth
         B: (. laughs) /you fancy it_'your`self `do you # -
         A: /`what # the /men's `'doubles #
         B: yeah (S.7.3.e4.4)

Part of the intervening material (turns five to seven) in this exchange is not concerned at all with the referent *the men's doubles*, and thus constitutes a kind of thematic break in the conversation. It is probably this qualitative difference which partially explains the problematic recoverability of the reparandum, since in quantitative terms the distance between the antecedent and the pronominal reparandum is not that large. This exchange shows once again that it would be wrong to try and analyze information flow in conversation in a linear, non-interactional manner.

7.3.3. Interference

We have already touched upon the third factor which can influence a referent's recoverability status, viz. interference. We have already shown that, even when there is a clearly recoverable, non-distant antecedent present in the preceding context, this does not always lead to unproblematic pronominalization; this is due to the potential presence of other candidates for coreference which "interfere" with straightforward coreference links.

There are a few clear examples of interference in our other-repair data, which are worth analyzing in some detail. The first one is (218) below:

(218)   *a: there are certain French maps much earlier than that*
          *I mean like early nineteenth **century ((like ours))***
          *A: **oh yes I mean the British** army ---*
          a: no I only meant that maps must have existed
          A: oh maps must have existed certainly - (coughs) oh the
          French would have mapped it very - carefully yes --
          well I mean this bears the mark of being a kind of
          independent survey doesn't it
          a: I know that's what's curious
          B: what you mean the English . aspect of it --- I believe it's
          a bit of an amalgam ((this map)) (S.2.3.8.5)

In the preceding context, explicit mention is made of both *the British*
and *the French*, so both are potential antecedents for the *that* in
speaker a's turn. Since the context does not give any unequivocal
clues as to which is the right coreference reading, the speaker seems
to have overdone Economy and thus endangered Clarity, which gives
rise to the hearer-repair in the last turn.

Another clear instance of interference from other candidates for
coreference (this time more than one) is (219) below:

(219)   *A: (...) we went to dine with Ken and *Carlotta -*
          *(-- laughs)**
          *B: *((oh)) - ((I)) believe* - James was entertaining Michael*
          A: yes that's right . m (. laughs)
          B: he's entertaining us on Friday I think
          *A: (--- laughs) hah - everybody individually *. m**
          *B: *don't tell* . Ken this # but /rumour 'has it that `he's .*
          [a/`bout to 'go #] # .
          A: "/`Ken is #
          B: yeah - (S.7.3.f15.4)

Instance (219) is interesting, in that the repair of *Ken* appears to be
due to interference from more than one other referent (cf. *James*,
Michael) in the immediately preceding context. The fact that the
intended antecedent, *Ken*, is the last mentioned preceding referent
does not appear to be a sufficient condition for establishing
unambiguous coreference. This shows once again that referent-
tracking is not achieved on a purely linear basis.

As a final example of interference resulting in an other-initiated other-repair, consider (220):

(220)   D: *well we can't fir . *fit the freezer* in **that's that's our problem***
        A: *((them both in))**
        B: **I can't fit . the** dishwasher *well I've got a little extension built on .
        D: *because . there ((really isn't the [s sə] **you know 2 sylls))** space on the wall ((that's the trouble))*
        A: **yeah well we we**
        B: ((5-6 sylls)) laundry but it's got a freezer in it*
        A: we're gonna have an **extension ((3-4 sylls))**
        D: **but when our extension** is done . we shall have space at the side and we shall *probably*
        C: *they /ought* to be out^side # /^anyway # /^oughtn't they #
        B: / `m #
        D: / `what # the / `freezer #
        C: the / `freezer # (...) (S.4.3.23.1)

Although the referent *the freezer* has been mentioned explictly before, there is a competing referent *the dishwasher* in the context, which apparently leads to comprehension problems for speaker D. Note, incidentally, that speaker B does *not* appear to have any problems processing the original anaphor; this shows that that it is not easy for the speaker to strike the right balance between Economy and Clarity, as it can be dependent on a variety of factors, such as shared background, the degree of attention the hearer is paying, etc.

7.4. Prosodic aspects of other-repairs

In this section, we will have a look at some intonational features of other-initiated other-repairs. Table 10 shows the final pitch movement of the reparandum utterance, i.e. just before initiation of the repair starts.

Since in other-initiated repairs, the repair is initiated by the fact that the hearer has an information flow problem, he will probably start initiating the repair even if the speaker has just uttered a floor-

start initiating the repair even if the speaker has just uttered a floor-holding cue, such as a final rising tone. In other words, not too much importance should be attached to the relatively high frequency of rising tones. For this reason, the intonation of other-repairs is interactionally less interesting, and is only summarized here for the sake of completeness.

Table 10. Intonation of other-initiated other-repairs

	absolute frequency	relative frequency
falling tone	7	(50.0%)
rising tone	5	(35.7%)
no tone / NS	2	(14.3%)
total	14	(100%)

7.5. Conclusion

This chapter completes the analysis of the different interactional types of anaphor repair, by looking at other-initiated other-repairs. First of all, our data show that the same pragmatic principles which we have discussed in chapters 3 and 4 are at work here; the repairs analyzed here find their explanation in the tension between the Economy principle and the Clarity principle. This shows that there is indeed some justification for regarding these principles as general pragmatic maxims dealing with the structuring of information in conversational discourse. Secondly, our findings here show that the tracking of referents in conversation is indeed a collaborative process, in which the hearer can play a very active role. By not only initiating the repair, but by also carrying out the correction, this collaborative dimension is even clearer in the other-repairs discussed in this chapter. These other-repairs also put our previous findings in chapters 3 and 4 in a broader perspective, since they show that the self-repairs reflected in RDs are indeed only part of a more general interactional phenomenon, the outcome of which is open to variation. Thirdly, and finally, the other-repairs discussed here provide evidence for the claim that the pragmatic tension apparent here appears to be due to the problematic recoverability status of the referent involved. This status is dependent on inferability, referential distance, or interference, or any combination of these three factors.

Chapter 8

Variant types of anaphor repair

8.1. Introduction

In this chapter, we will discuss various types of repair which are all, in some way or other, related to the self- and other-repairs analyzed in chapters 3, 4 and 7; their common denominator is the fact that they are all repairs through which a pragmatically underspecified pronominal form is replaced by a more informational, full lexical reference form (mostly an NP). These repairs, however, all fail to meet one or more of the criteria for qualifying as RDs; at the most, they can be regarded as RD-related phemomena.

We will try to make several points here. First of all, by showing that there are classes of repair which are hard to categorize in terms of them being RDs, we will show that the linguistic category of RD defies strict categorization. We have already discussed borderline cases at previous points (notably in chapter 6), but the phenomena discussed here illustrate even more clearly the point that the category "RD" shows prototypical organization on several levels. They also show that the decision what to regeard as a clear RD and what not must necessarily be somewhat arbitrary, due to the very nature of RD itself.

Secondly, we will attempt to make an important related point about the nature of RD. We have claimed in chapter 6 that (repair-) RD is not merely a syntactic construction, but rather a reflection of an interactional process. It is, we have claimed, nothing more than the, in a sense accidental, outcome of such a process. If such processes indeed take place, one could imagine that they may have other potential outcomes, RD being only one among a range of possibilities (albeit perhaps a favoured one, in the sense that it is, after all, an instantiation of self-initiated self-repair). The findings in this chapter show that this is indeed the case, i.e. the interactional repair process discussed earlier may be realized in a variety of other ways besides

RD. Indirectly, then, the analysis in this chapter confirms our claims about the processual, interactional nature of RD.

A third point, and perhaps the most inportant one, which we want to make in this chapter is the fact that our findings on RD-related repairs show the pragmatic principles of Clarity and Economy (cf. chapter 2) to be non–ad-hoc. That is to say, they can be shown to be also at work in the repairs discussed here, and thus to have general applicability. The fact that they appear to be at work not just in cases of RD-like repairs but also in other contexts is in fact good evidence that they may indeed be, as we have claimed, general principles of information management in conversation, and perhaps in discourse in general.

Fourthly, the findings in this chapter, we hope, show that the concept of recoverability, which was introduced for analyzing the informational status of referents in RDs, is applicable to other phenomena besides clear RDs. Indeed, we will try to show that the repairs discussed here often originate in the problematic recoverability status of the reparandum.

Three types of repair will be discussed. In 8.2, we will discuss instances in which the reparans (to which we will go on referring as the REF, for convenience' sake) is not a bare NP, but is embedded in some clausal framework (usually consisting of a repetition of part of the PROP). Section 8.3 deals with other forms of pronoun-to-noun repair, mostly of the type in which the pronominal gap gets repaired immediately, as opposed to at the end of a complete clause (needless to say, such repairs tend to be self-initiated and self-correcting, as we will see below). Section 8.4 discusses repairs in which the reparandum is some linguistically "empty" category (labelled "Ø"), such as a zero anaphor. In section 8.5, finally, we will look at some prosodic aspects of all these variant anaphor repairs.

8.2. Retracing anaphor repairs

8.2.1. Different types

In this section, we will investigate repairs in which part of the original utterance centaining the reparandum is repeated; these repairs are thus to some extent "retracing" repairs (Van Wijk 1987). A first type of repair, and one which closely resembles RD, is the one in

which the main verb of the PROP is repeated together with the REF;
e.g.:

(221)   A: *how's the thesis going*
         B: *[ə] /I'm typing <u>it</u> 'up `now # . /typing up <u>the final</u>*
         A: *[hm]*
         B: *'copy #*
         A: *[ə] when are you submitting it (S.2.1.1.6)*

The REF *the final copy* clearly repairs the pronoun *it* in the previous
clause; what keeps the structure from being classified as a RD,
however, is the fact that the PROP-verb *typing* is repeated along
with the reparans. We would claim that the difference between such
structures, which we might call (following Van Wijk 1987) "tensed
verb reduplications", and proper RDs is in fact a marginal one.
Indeed, the difference between (221) and the potential repair (222),
which does qualify as a RD, is not very outspoken:

(222)   *I'm typing it up now . the final copy.*

This is a very good argument in favour of our claim that RD is, as it
were, the accidental outcome of a repair process, for structures like
(221) suggest that interactionally very similar repairs may or may not
surface as RDs, depending on such formal factors as verb
reduplication, which are in fact relatively unimportant form a
functional point of view. Depending on how narrowly one delineates
one's definition of "central" RDs, instances such as (221) thus just
fall inside or outside the borderline, which again shows the prototype
properties of RD. Let us just mention two similar instances, just to
show that (221) is not an isolated case:

(223)   A: *(...) -- Randall's in the book # . ((you)) /find <u>him</u> [f]*
              /find '<u>Randall's</u> `'name # /in the /in the `book a'bout
              'Ulster # that the /[aiə] Sunday ^Times 'wrote # (...)
              (S.1.14.a68.8)

(224)   [context: about organization of lectures]
         B: *he certainly ought to consider that -*
         A: *well . *you**
         B: *we've* had rather [ə:] - . you know without giving too*

> *much away to ((3-4 sylls))*
> *A: yeah # . well he's /got a [`very good 'bloke] doing it*
> *`now # . I /-mean # /doing this `'organizing # Godfrey*
> *Campion . [ə:] (...) (S.5.11.a35.2)*

Both are instances of reduplication of the main verb in the PROP
(*find* and *doing*, respectively). Note the overt repair-initiator *I mean*
in (224).

There are a few instances where the REF is even more embedded
in a clausal framework, in that it is not only accompanied by a
repetition of the main verb of the PROP, but also by a repetition of its
subject argument; e.g.:

(225)   *A: . yes # but /this is something I `want # /one day I want*
         a `room # where a /`sewing machine # /stands `up #
         /`permanently # . (S.1.3.12.11)

The REF *a room where...* is in fact the object of the repeated subject-
verb sequence *I want,* which also occurs in the PROP. This is a bit
like the tensed verb reduplications mentioned above, but even less
RD-related, in that the REF is part of a self-contained clause. Some
other instances:

(226)   *C: (...) --- [əm] - /he gives "some of them in this `room # -*
         his /`undergraduate 'ones # he /gives in this `room #
         (...) (S.1.5.59.11)

(227)   *B: wasn't very far way . it might have been Belsize Park*
         A: /oh well that's 'where his `mother 'lives # . /mother
         'lives at 'Belsize `park # (...) (S.1.6.12.1)

(228)   *B: (...) - . /will you 'feel that you'll 'do it when it's your*
         `own # I /-mean # [w] /when it's your 'own # will
         you /feel sort of you 'want to "do a con'version #
         (S.2.10.123.7)

In the following instance, reparans (*those stories*) and reparandum
(*him*) do not agree in number and gender:

(229)   *B: ((2 sylls)) do you /`'like him # . do you `'like those*
               'stories #
         A: (...) (S.3.5.a11.5)

It is clear from the context that this is indeed an appropriateness
repair rather than an error repair; (229) thus belongs in the same class
as (225-228).

Instance (230) is slightly different from the ones mentioned
above, in that the PROP-verb is not really repeated:

(230)   *A: (...) . and it was /[∂:m] - (and)) there are /only about*
              [?] `'twenty of these # a "/`year # . oc/cur a `year #
              ((of the)) par/ticular `problem I 'had # - (...)
              (S.2.9.1.6)

In this repair, the speaker, on top of providing the reparans *the
particular problem I had*, decides also to change the main verb of the
PROP, and replace it with *occur*. The result is a reparans which is a
verbal argument; unlike the previous cases, however, we are not
dealing with verb reduplication. Nevertheless, (230) appears to be
very similar to (222-224) above.

Finally, there is an instance of an argument-REF which differs
somewhat from the previous cases:

(231)   *A: I /`'like 'that # do you /mean this the /second one a'long #*
              /`'yes # I /like 'that # - (S.1.8.75A.3)

The REF *the second one along* here is, strictly speaking, an
argument (i.e. the object) of *do you mean;* the latter, however, has
the status of being the repair-initiating expression. It could be argued
that the REF is not really the object of *mean*, since this functions on
an entirely different level, as a discourse signal. Note, incidentally,
that this repair has an element of other-correction, for it is very likely
(cf. the *yes* in A's turn) that the REF, which is tentatively suggested
by the speaker, is extralinguistically confirmed by the hearer.

8.2.2. Information flow

This section briefly attempts to show that, firstly, the repairs discussed in the previous section are also due to the clash between C- and E-principle, and that, secondly, this clash can be accounted for in terms of the problematic recoverability status of the reparandum-referent.

First of all, the reparandum in these repairs, just as is the case in repair-RDs, is a pronominal form, that is to say, a semantically unspecified form. Such forms are on the one hand economical (the E-principle), in that it is the most minimal form the speaker can use for a referent whose reference is clear from the context. On the other hand, however, such minimal forms do run the risk of not being informative enough (violation of the C-principle), in that the hearer may be unable to establish unambiguous reference. The pronominal form may thus be pragmatically underspecified, and in need of repair.

There are various reasons why the pronoun-gap may fail to meet the informativeness standards required for the speech situation, and thus be pragmatically underspecified. In (221) for instance, repeated here as (232), the reparandum is only indirectly inferable from the context:

(232)   *A: how's the thesis going*
        B: [ə] /I'm typing <u>*it*</u> *'up ˋnow # . /typing up* <u>*the final*</u>
        A: [hm]
        B: <u>*ˊcopy*</u> *# (S.2.1.1.6)*

The speaker here has made an inferential jump from *the thesis* to *the final copy (of the thesis)*, a jump which the hearer might be unable to work out. In instance (226), repeated here as (233), we have a contrastive context, which leaves the gap *some of them* ambiguous:

(233)   *C: (...) --- [əm] - /he gives "*<u>*some of them*</u> *in this ˋroom # -*
        his /ˋundergraduate 'ones # he /gives in this ˋroom #
        (...) (S.1.5.59.11)

Since the gap might refer to either member of the contrast pair, a repair is advisable, to ensure adequate informativeness. Instance

(231), repeated here as (234), is a case of extralinguistic rather than linguistic inferability:

(234)   *A: I / `like 'that # do you /mean this the /second one a 'long #*
         I 'yes # I /like 'that # - (S.1.8.75A.3)

The referent *the second one along* is just one in a series of extralinguistically available referents, and thus prone to confusion if left pronominalized.

We should point out, however, that sometimes a repair occurs when the reparandum appears to be unproblematic; instance (227), repeated here as (235), is a case in point:

(235)   *B: wasn't very far way . it might have been Belsize Park*
         A: /oh well that's 'where his `mother 'lives # . /mother
         'lives at 'Belsize `park # (...) (S.1.6.12.1)

The REF *Belsize Park* is directly recoverable from the previous turn, so the reparandum can hardly be called ambiguous here. It would appear, then, that the speaker can opt to be more informative than is really necessary, and provide a repair where none is really needed, thus violating the E-principle somewhat. After all, violating the E-principle is in some ways the lesser of two evils, since in most cases it does not lead to ineffective reference establishment, but merely to redundancy

8.3. Immediate anaphor repairs

8.3.1. Interactional aspects

This section deals with repairs which are carried out immediately rather than at the end of the completed clause (i.e. the TRP). As a starting-point, let us consider a few instances of the type of repair we will be discussing here:

(236)   *A: yet I [st] as far as I know it's just a particular type*
         of stout which the Irish developed # because of
         that marvellous water they've got # . /so you `'really
         they # . the /`Irishmen 'say # there's /no such `thing

> as the 'true thing in 'England # because it's the water .
> (S.1.7.40.5)

(237)   A: (...) I wouldn't be able to have that one # for /some
'reason you see . "/ `this # . the / `checkerboard effect
- [ə:m] I re/coil " `badly from 'this # (...)
(S.1.8.91.7)

(238)   B: (...) . why on earth ((did I forget)) ((3 sylls)) ((Thursday
night or something --- I don't know why I missed it #
it's a /bit)) --- /eight ` `ten's # a /bit - a /bit too `early
for 'me # ((/ `isn't it)) .
c: m   (S.1.11.a20.4)

In (236), for instance, the pronominal reparandum *they* is replaced
by the full lexical NP *the Irishmen;* similarly, in (237) and (238),
this is repaired by means of *this checkerboard effect,* and *it* by *eight
ten,* respectively. In all, there are 37 instances of this kind of
pronoun-to-NP repair in our database.

There are two things worth noting about the repairs in this section.
First of all, all of these are self-initiated, self-correcting repairs,
which is hardly surprising. For one thing, other-initiation usually
only occurs at an outspoken TRP, i.e. at the end of a clause, whereas
the repairs discussed here are clause-internal. Therefore, if a repair is
other-initiated, it tends to turn up either as a RD format (if it is self-
correcting; cf. chapter 4), or as an other-initiated, other-correcting
repair (cf chapter 7). Repairs which are self-initiated and other-
correcting are very rare, as we have pointed out before; if the speaker
himself initiates a repair, he is likely to also carry out correction.

Secondly, most of these repairs are immediate repairs, i.e. there is
no delay, but the reparans comes immediately following or closely
after the reparandum. This is to be expected; after all, if repair is
delayed until after the end of the clause, the result will in most cases
be a RD format (cf. chapter 3) or a related format (cf. the previous
section). Examples of repairs which immediately follow the
reparandum are (236) and (237) above, and (239) to (242) below:

(239)   C: (...) - I personally would not like [ə:] to know # .
ex/actly what this good `lady # . [ə:] ex/pected her

the "`wife of a family # to /give them to `eat # - (...)
(S.5.4.37.11)

(240) M: (...) . it [? ?] /that `phrase # . /quoted there # is a
       /consolation phrase # for the sur/`vivors # (...)
       (S.5.2.20.1)

(241) A: (...) --- it / `is 'similar # in /that dra`´matic 'sense #
       /that it the /circumstance pre`´dominates # - (...)
       (S.3.5.b58.8)

(242) B: (...) and I /think this is the `way 'they . /England
       "`copes # /is the fact that we `never # -- we /[nev]
       we /aren't a 'militaristic 'nation # -- (...) (S.2.3.53.7)

In all these cases, the reparans occurs right after the reparandum.
    Instances of slightly delayed repairs, which are not delayed as far
as the end of the clause, are (238) above, and (243) to (245) below:

(243) A: (...) --- and /this as I / `say # /this . [th] this `fellowship
       # is a "/ `two year ´thing # and it goes in rotation round
       the women's colleges - (...) (S.1.3.59.7)

(244) A: (...) - /he said [?] . the /other 'chap ¯said # .`/ `you know
       # /have I 'had enough `time # there were / `´three of
       them you 'see # (...) (S.2.9.10.8)

(245) A: well what did they look like did they `look like sheep's
          eyes -
       B: well they "/ `´smell the /dish "/ `´smelt /absolutely
          re"`volting # (...) (S.4.6.b8.6)

In most of these cases, repair is initiated right after the finite verb,
which is then repeated after the reparans.
    Once again, repairs such as these show that RD is only one of the
possible realizations of the interactional repair process. After all,
these repairs are functionally very similar to self-initiated RD-repairs,
the only difference being the location of the repair-initiation (clause-

internal rather than clause- final). The next section shows that there are other similarities.

8.3.2. Information flow

The repairs discussed here, we argue, resemble RD-repairs, in that the reparandum has a problematic recoverability status, due to the clash between the Economy (E-) and the Clarity (C-) principles. Our discussion will be relatively brief, in that we will restrict ourselves to an analysis of a few selected instances.

The following, first of all, is a clear instance of an inferable REF:

(246)   A: *and you're [?] . now engaged - in [ə:] . in preparing*
                a book on him .
            B: **((mhm . that's right yes))**
            A: **in the meantime* you're writing on various discrete*
                aspects of Piggott in the form of articles and that
                kind of thind and *that's been going on for
                some while*
            B: **[ə:] --**
            A: ***((1 syll))***
            B: ***well #** they /started the /chapters 'tended to start in*
                the 'form of `articles # (...) (S.3.6.46.2)

The referent *the chapters* here is indirectly inferable from *a book* and *articles* in the immediately preceding context. However, since the speaker cannot be sure that his original pronominal reference form will be correctly interpreted, he replaces the more economical form (the pronoun) by means of a more informative one (a full NP). The following also have inferable REFs:

(247)   A: *[ə:m] . I /think it's quite worth seeing*
            B: *m*
            A: *but I certainly [ə ə] you know # one has rather mixed*
                feelings # I in [ə] - an /`odd 'sort of `way # /`some of
                them # [?ə] the "/`actors I 'thought # were a /bit sort
                of "`amateurish #
            B: *(...) (S.7.1.c9.2)*

(248)   A: [ðm] -- but it it's a bit un`nerving # you I `know # ((there
          were)) /situ`'ations # where oc/casionally I'd say
          something `funny # --- and /five people would `laugh
          # . and `I'd laugh # and /these `two # *-- the
          phi/`losophy lady #*
          B: *(--- laughs)*
          A: and the /other [`nameless] `subjectless lady # - /just sat
          and `stared at me # - (...) (S.1.3.28.3)

In (247), *the actors* is inferable from the *it* in the first turn, which
refers to *a play;* in (248), *the philosophy lady...* is inferable from the
entire prior context.

   Problematic recoverability may follow from other factors. The
following is an instance of interference:

(249)   A: (...) and . my friends in . King's University Tyrone - .
          introduced me my father's friends there professor of
          classics professor Weddleborough - a great . yachts-
          man . [s] oh [s] sailed up the [ʃæni] Shannon with
          my father

          b: m .

          A: my father having learnt yachting in Dublin harbour . as
          a [tsh] [tsh] as a as a boy # -- sailing was their great
          thing # . and `they # - the /Weddle `boroughs # /told
          [ð] . I /I found /I the /Weddle`boroughs started
          `'talking to 'me (...) (S.1.14.a97.7)

The reparandum *they* in this context might or might not include *my
father;* the reparans *the Weddleboroughs* makes clear that it does
not. Note that this instance is also inferable, in that there is an
inferential jump from the singular *professor Weddleborough* to the
plural *the Weddleboroughs.*

   The following, finally, is an example of problematic recoverability
due to the referent being referentially distant (the REF *banging on the
ceiling* being mentioned five turns earlier):

(250)   A: and how she ((heard)) repeated . bangs on the ceiling -
          [5 turns with 27 tone units intervening]

> B: (...) I mean <u>it</u> / `could # <u>this "/ `banging on [the / `ceiling</u> #]
> # could have been /water in the `pipes # or or the
> /central `heating or something # (...) (S.5.8.39.3)

It should be pointed out once again that sometimes the reparandum is, at first sight, unproblematic, but the speaker nevertheless chooses to initiate a repair; the following is an example of this:

(251)   B: (...) she caught [∂:m] - I don't know if it was pleurisy or
         something - but I imagine that was because she wasn't
         heating the house properly # [∂:m] - /oh it /<u>it</u> was I
         mean <u>the / `house</u> # . we /used to go 'over `'often
         e'nough # to . I mean it /wasn't in 'any `state # (...)
         (S.5.8.108.7)

The REF *the house* is directly recoverable from the previous tone unit. The speaker thus errs on the side of over-informativeness rather than risking being too economical. Such instances, however, are exceptional.

8.3.3. First and second person repairs

There are two classes of pronoun-to-NP repairs which are quite unlike any of the ones encountered before, in that the reparandum is not a third person, but either a first or second person pronoun.

First of all, let us consider instances in which the gap is the first person plural pronoun *we*. This pronoun is inherently ambiguous: it refers to the speaker and one or more other people, who may or not be present in the speech situation. In some cases, where the precise identity of the referents referred to is important, one might thus imagine *we* being insufficiently informative. There are indeed several such cases in our data; let us first consider an instance is some detail:

(252)   C: well . /well you see # . /<u>we</u> all 'went to this `poetry
         'reading it 'was # / '<u>Ian</u> # and / 'me and # <u>and</u>
         / `<u>Neil</u> 'wasn't it # /-and [∂:] # - <u>and / `Martin</u> # -
         (...) (S.2.7.72.5)

In this instance, the speaker obviously wants to make clear the exact reference of *we*, and thus lists all referents (besides the speaker herself: *Ian, Neal,* and *Martin*) in full lexical guise. Some other instances, all of the same type:

(253)   A: *have you not approached anybody else*
         B: */and [∂] we are - we "/both [∂:] ((Joe and I both*
             Eccleston)) and my`self # /have `fellowships to
             the `Elworthy . [/`library [in /O`hio [this
             /`summer #] #] # - (...) (S.2.1.18.1)

(254)   A: *(...) and . I've got /`postcards ((at home)) # which*
             /Thomas `sent us [to the /`children #] # (...)
             (S.5.8.62.1)

(255)   B: *we've got to give Northern Ireland . people themselves*
             sitting down together the chance to work out that
             policy # . which /`we # - /[thi:] Westminster
             `Parliament # must /then . `rule `on # . (S.6.2.31.6)

The following category consists of instances in which the reparandum is a second person pronoun. This type of pronouns is also ambiguous in certain speech situations, in that it refers to the hearer or hearers; if there are, however, more than two participants, there are several candidates for the reference of *you,* i.e. any number of participants between one and the total number of hearers. Such an ambiguity is present, for instance, in the following, where the original *you* does not unambiguously signal that the speaker means *all four of you:*

(256)   F: *(...) and /I think [∂] you've all "`four of `you # .*
             /given your `own # . sub/`jective re`actions # to
             /three of these [∂] . four phe`nomena # (...)
             (S.5.2.11.13)

The following is slightly different, in that the speaker here wants *you* to encompass both the hearer and a third party:

(257)   B: */yeah but `you've /you and your [`students] are*
             "`sharing # a /great `deal al`ready # (...) (S.5.7.11.7)

The following, finally, is different still; there is no real ambiguity here, since *you* clearly refers to *the Prime Minister:*

(258)   *A: by the autumn Prime Minister you'll have to have*
           something to . put in the place of the Conservative
           Phase Three # - /how is [`your] `mind # /how is
           the `government's `mind # . / `moving on 'that at
           the 'moment # - (S.6.3.62.9)

However, since the speaker wants to address him in his "persona" of leader of *the government,* he considers the pronoun not to be adequately informative.

8.4. Repairs from   linguistic zero-forms ("Ø") to NP

8.4.1. Semantic types

This section deals with repairs through which a linguistically absent element becomes specified. There are a number of types of Ø-to-NP repairs which ought to be distinguished, if one wants to get a clear semantic picture. Four different classes will be discussed in turn.

First of all, sometimes a Ø > NP repair introduces a modifier to a NP which previously did not have one; this is the case, for instance, in (259):

(259)   *A: what had you been doing all that time .*
           B: /I did some ⁀work # -
           A: on -
           B: /my `thesis # --
           A: jolly good (S.2.1.a7.2)

The reparandum here is *work Ø*, a NP which gets the NP-modifier *on my thesis* attached to it as a reparans. Similar instances are (260) and (261):

(260)   *b: (...) while we were in India - we saw the programme .*
           about -
           *C: /ah `yes # Pe/nelope's `friend *in'deed # . on the box*
           *exactly**

A: *oh Geoffrey Lardner on the spactics* **yes yes**
b: **that's right on spastics** (...) (S.2.14.66.10)

(261)   B: good . well on your [d] domestic front how's the house
         C: oh God *foul*
         B: *are* [j j] are you decorating [hə] have you done what
             you . you threatened to do start [əm] . painting
             and god knows what
         C: I `well # [əm] /I'm 'still 'trying to 'do . I'm e/`mulsion
             'painting # <u>the /bit 'round the `top</u> #
         B: /top of `what #
         C: be/fore we 'hang the `paper #
         B: the /top of
         C: /<u>of the `dining 'room</u> #
         B: this is the dining room that you stripped
         C: yes - (...) (S.7.1.a39.11)

These are both instances of NP-modifying repairs.

A second type introduces an adverbial, where no such adverbial is present in the original utterance; this adverbial usually sets the PROP in some temporal or spatial framework. Some examples:

(262)   A: /do you in 'fact 'usually 'bother to '<u>eat</u> at * ´all #*
         D: */`no #* - I mean <u>at lunch</u> yes # (...) (S.1.5.77.1)

(263)   c: you're flying home aren't you .
         A: m . I'm /<u>sending</u> a couple of tin `trunks # /full of `gear
             through #
         b: that's the way
         c: what <u>by sea</u> *((you mean))*
         A: */`m #* - (S.1.10.100.3)

(264)   C: you /know we <u>did</u> `Latin [ə:] for our ´English # -
         B: I `yes # --- */`m #*
         C: *and* /Roman `history [as I `well #] # .
         B: I `what # [æ?] <u>in I`´college</u> # **or at I`school # I`m #**
         C: **((in college)) -** (...) (S.2.5.a56.8)

The reparanda here are a time, manner, and place adverbial, respectively.

A third type are more or less clear zero-anaphors, i.e. a linguistically unrealized pronoun which is replaced by an NP; e.g.:

(265)   B: *that `green is /not ´bad # / `is it # that /`´land'scape* #
         A: *what the bright one - *((its))**
         B: *yes *well it's* not very bright (...) (S.1.8.7.3)*

The reparandum *that green Ø* is replaced here by *landscape;* the reparandum is obviously very similar to *that green one* (in which case we would have had an instantiation of RD). Other instances are:

(266)   B: *but you can't see both of them can you [them = films]*
         A: *((well /if)) **it's the 'same `'price #***
         B: ***I /mean there are two /are there** 'two `´screens
            *[at the /ABC 'Shaftesbury ´Avenue #] #**
         c: *oh sorry . yes no no no . no* you're right . yes . yes
            they are -- (S.2.10.82.4)*

(267)   B: *(...) but /how do I move the `hands # does /that . /does
            that [∂] `´face # /spring ´off # .*
         A: */ `no # / `no # you /look on the ⌐back # . [∂:m] . [th∂] if
            /you 'look . (. coughs)*
         B: *the /[`three] little `´brown # . [th] the /`´screw things # .*
         A: */no `no # [∂:] [i] [∂] [∂:m] if /you 'just ´((turn)) /you
            /which 'clock do you `mean # the *e/`lectric 'one #***
         B: **the e/`lectric #* . / ´yeah #*
         A: */ `well # you /hook you /un´hook it # . (...) (S.7.2.d7.7)*

The reparanda here are are both instances of zero-anaphors.

Finally, there is one interesting instance in which the PROP is a passive sentence without a BY-phrase, and in which the reparans consists of precisely that BY-phrase, specifying the agent of the main verb:

(268)   A: *(...) it's /often been - `criticised # ((the /´way #)) that
            it's /just*
         B: ***by /`whom # -- /by `whom #***
         A: ***. im´mediately . [/slipped `in #] # -** - [∂:m] ---
            I /don't think I'm thinking of the `modern .
            ´critics . [for /´that #] # . [∂:m] - ((/´there #)) ---*

B: / `who # ---
A: ((I)) don't re`member an 'actual . [kri] 'critic #
   (S.3.5.b44.5)

Note that the reference is not really provided, as speaker A fails to come up with a referent for the BY-phrase.

8.4.2. Interactional types

This section will discuss Ø-to-NP repairs from the point of view of self- versus other-initiation and self- versus other-correction. First of all, it should be pointed out that all four interactional types of repair are represented in the data, with the following frequencies:

(269)   self-initiated self-repair: 4 (26.5%)
         other-initiated self-repair: 7 (46.5%)
         self-initiated other-repair: 1 (7.0%)
         other-initiated other-repair: 3 (20.0%)

The most striking tendency emerging from this is the fact that there appears to be a preference for other-initiation (two thirds of the data) over-self-initiation (one third); such a preference is quite exceptional.

Given the nature of these data, however, we claim that this is not really that surprising, and is even in line with what one might expect. Indeed, it must be borne in mind that, in most cases, the reparandum utterance is in fact already very informational. From the speaker's point of view, there is no reason to believe that he may have violated the C-principle; he thus sees no need to self-initiate a repair. Contrary to what can be expected, the hearer does feel that he has not received sufficient information, and thus in most cases it is the hearer rather than the speaker who will feel the need to initiate a repair. Hence the preference for other- over self-initiation here.

If our reasoning is valid, then one would expect there to be one class of repairs which deviates from this pattern. Indeed, in those repairs where a zero-anaphor is replaced by a full noun, the speaker is more likely to have violated the C-principle. One would thus expect self-initiation to be more expected in such cases. This is indeed borne out by the data: of the five repairs in this category (cf. also the previous section), four are self-initiated; there is only one exception. The special nature of these repairs thus indirectly confirms our claim about the other-initiation preference of the other-repairs discussed in this section.

Having established this, we can now have a closer look at the data. The self-initiated, self-correcting repairs in the data are instances (265) to (267) above; we have already pointed out that they are zero-anaphor repairs.

Self-initiated, other-correcting repairs, as we have pointed out already on other occasions, are very rare, since the speaker, once he has initiated the repair, is also the most natural candidate for correcting the reparandum. The only instance of self-initiated other-repair is (260) above. The reparandum, i.e. the NP-modifier *about* Ø, is started by the speaker, but in fact repaired jointly by the two other participants.

Other-initiated, other-correcting repairs are not very frequent. We will have a closer look at one instance, viz. (263), repeated here as (270):

(270)   *c: you're flying home aren't you .*
     A: m . I'm /sending a couple of tin `trunks # /full of `gear
        through #
     b: that's the way
     c: what by sea *((you mean))*
     A: */`m #* - (S.1.10.100.3)

The reparans *by sea* is both initiated (cf. *what*) and uttered by one of the hearers here. Note the fact that the speaker acknowledges the other-reparans provided, so that we get the following interactional sequence:

(271)   step 1: (speaker) utterance with reparandum
     step 2: (hearer) initiation of repair + correction (reparans)
     step 3: (speaker) acknowledgment of reparans

We have argued, and will argue, elsewhere that this acknowlegment-step is an essential ingredient in the process of other-repairs.

Finally, we can turn to the most frequently occurring type of repairs, viz. other-initiated self-repairs. There are no less than 7 instances in our data. Instances (272) and (273) are worth looking into, as they are somewhat special:

(272)   A: (...) # - . [ə:m] /what's 'his position in the de`partment
              'now # -
        B: /as regards his 'teaching #
        A: [ə] /`no # his /`job # -
        B: his /`what #
        A: his /`job # .
        B: well (...) (S.5.11.a36.6)

What is interesting about (272) is the fact that there is an attempt at
other-correction, which is, however, unsuccessful. Note also that the
first attempt by the speaker is not successful, so he has to provide the
reparans a second time. A hint of other-correction also occurs in
(273):

(273)   C: you /know we did `Latin [ə:] for our 'English # -
        B: /`yes # --- */`m #*
        C: *and* /Roman `history [as /`well #] # .
        B: /`what # [æ?] in /`college # **or at /`school # /`m #**
        C: **((in college)) -** (...) (S.2.5.a56.8)

In this instance, the hearer, after initiating the repair, limits the range
of reparanda down to just two possibilities.

8.5. Prosodic aspects of variant anaphor repairs

We will very briefly discuss three prosodic features here: the
occurrence of pauses and/or turns, the occurrence of tone unit
boundaries between reparandum and reparans, and the pitch
movement prior to repair-initiation.

Table 11. Occurrence of pauses/turns in variant anaphor repairs

	retracing	immed.	Ø-to-NP	total	
[+ turn]	—	—	11	11	(17.8%)
[+ pause]	08	16	02	26	(41.9%)
[- pause]	02	21	02	25	(40.3%)
total	10	37	15	62	(100%)

Table 11 shows the occurrence of pauses or turns between reparandum and repair-initiation, in all three types of pronoun-to-NP repair. These figures show that almost two thirds of the data have either a pause or a turn (or both) between reparandum and reparans. These reflect, respectively, self-initiation (possibly tacitly other-prompted) and other-initiation of the repair.

Table 12. Tonality of variant anaphor repairs

	retracing	immed.	Ø-to-NP	total	
[+ #]	09	24	14	47	(75.8%)
[- #]	01	13	01	15	(24.2%)
total	10	37	15	62	(100 %)

Table 12 shows the tonality of repair-related RDs, more specifically the occurrence of tone unit boundaries between reparandum and reparans. The figures show that, in most cases, there is indeed such a tone unit boundary, resulting in the reparans having its own separate nucleus or nuclei. In instances where this is not the case, i.c. in quite a number of immediate pronoun-to-NP repairs, this is due to the fact that it is the reparandum (which is thus an unstressed pronoun) rather than the reparans which does not have a nuclear accent. In fact, in nearly all cases the reparans is marked by such an accent.

Table 13. Intonation of variant anaphor repairs

	retracing	immed.	Ø-NP	total	
falling	04	13	08	25	(40.3%)
rising	05	10	04	19	(30.7%)
no tone	01	14	03	18	(29.0%)
total	10	37	15	62	(100 %)

Table 13, finally, shows the final pitch movement of the reparandum utterance, i.e. just before initiation of the repair. These figure show a rather low frequency of falling tones (contrasting with the situation in repair-RDs). However, it must be kept in mind that, in quite a number of cases, repair is initiated before the end of a complete clause is reached (for instance, in all the PRO-to-NP repairs), so the rising tone there may be merely a turn-holding cue. The figures for intonation are thus of rather limited value here compared to those for repair-RDs.

8.6. Conclusion

This chapter has provided evidence that the functioning of RD as self-repair is not just an isolated phenomenon. On the contrary, we have tried to show that repairs of the RD type fit into a larger overall picture of various classes of informativeness repairs, which all resemble RD-repairs to a greater or lesser degree. In discussing these, we have established independent evidence that RD is obly one possible instantiation of a repair process motivated by the clash between two pragmatic principles, viz. Economy and Clarity.

Some repairs discussed here formally differ from RD, in that the reparans is not "bare", but embedded in a clausal framework (cf. 8.2). Others are different in that the repair does not occur at the end of a complete clause, but is immediate, the "PROP" thus being incomplete (cf. 8.3). Finally, some repairs do not have an overt pronoun in the PROP, but have an even more minimal reparandum, viz. a linguistically empty form (cf. 8.4). Whether we still regard some of these as RDs is besides the point; rather, the existence of such structures shows once again that RD is hard to delineate categorially, and that some cases are clearly more central than others. Exact boundaries are thus impossible to draw, due to the very nature . of the RD process.

Chapter 9

Repairs of non-pronominal forms

9.1. Introduction

In this chapter, we will attempt to show that the repair mechanism we have outlined, and which is triggered by the clash between two pragmatic principles, in not restricted to repairs of a pronominal form by means of a full lexical NP. In showing the more general application of our pragmatic principles, we hope to prove that they are not ad hoc principles merely relevant for dealing with one specific class of data, viz. self-repairs or RDs (in fact, the previous chapter has already shown their wider applicability to some extent). On the contrary, we are dealing with general conversational principles of referential informativeness.

By discussing these non-pronominal referential repairs, we also try to show that anaphor repairs are not an isolated phenomenon, but part of a more general strategy through which informational trouble-spots are "corrected", by means of a co-operative effort between speaker and hearer. We have already shown, in the previous chapters, that RDs and other anaphor repairs are, as it were, only accidental outcomes of a PRO-to-NP repair process; in this chapter, we will show this process to be an instantiation of an even more general process through which a referentially inappropriate reference form is replaced by a more specific one.

The bulk of this chapter deals with the repairing of a fully lexical reference form (realized as an NP) by means of another fully lexical reference form (also an NP) which is in some way more specific, and thus more informational. This type of referential repair is fairly common: no fewer than 108 clear instances were found in the data. First of all, we will look at these from an interactional point of view (self- and other-initiation, self- and other-correction); we will show that all four interactional types of repair are represented in the database (9.2). Secondly, we will classify them on a formal basis

(9.3), by looking at the precise form of both reparandum and reparans. Thirdly, we will discuss the status of NP-to-NP repairs (9.4) with regard to information flow, and investigate why they are seen as violating the C-principle. Fourthly, and finally, we will look at some prosodic characteristics of these repairs (9.5), more particularly at the occurrence of prosodic boundaries, and at their intonation.

The final part of this chapter (9.6) deals with a variety of other reference forms, e.g. the repair of an NP by means of a full clause, etc. Since most referential forms are expressed by NPs (pronominal or lexical), this type of repair is relatively rare (there are a mere 26 instances in our data). We have used the label "X-to-X' repair to refer to this category.

9.2. Interactional types of NP-to-NP repair

First of all, it should be noted that all four interactional types of repair (self- and other-repair resulting from both self- and other-initiation) are realized in our data. Our data show a marked tendency towards self- over other-initiation, and towards self- over other-correction, resulting in self-initiated self-repair being the most frequently occurring repair type:

(274	self-initiated self-repair	79	(73%)
	other-initiated self-repair	16	(15%)
	self-initiated other-repair	1	(1%)
	other-initiated other-repair	11	(10%)
	other-initiated other- + self-repair	1	(1%)
	total number of NP-to-NP	108	(100%)

Almost three quarters of our corpus thus consists of self-initiated self-repair, which is in line with the findings of Schegloff—Jefferson—Sacks (1977), and with our own findings in previous chapters about referential repair.

9.2.1. Self-initiated self-repair

Let us now turn to some examples of each repair type. We will start off with instances of self-initiated self-repair; the first one of which will be discussed in detail:

(275)   A: *I'm "/still re"lying on "[`some of]* <u>*Kalapandy's `notes*</u> *# .*
        <u>*/notes I 'took of his `lectures*</u> *# - (...) (S.1.6.113.4)*

The speaker here utters a noun which is modified by a genitive, realizes it may not be informational enough, and repairs it by means of the same noun to which he now adds a relative modifying clause containing more information on the initial referent. Note that the speaker pauses after the reparandum; this occurs quite frequently (cf. also 9.5), and is reminiscent of the pauses occurring between PROP and REF in repair-RDs (cf. chapter 4). Note also that the "PROP" ends in a falling tone, a factor which probably has interactional relevance (cf. 9.5). An informational reason for the repair here may be the fact that the referent *Kalapandy's notes* is ambiguous, in that it could refer to either *notes made by Kalapandy of his lectures* or *notes I made of his lectures* (cf.9.4); the reparans makes clear that the speaker intends it to mean the latter. The informational trouble-spot again shows that the speaker, despite the fact that he has used a full lexical NP, has violated the C-principle. We thus see that informational inappropriateness is not restricted to pronouns.

    There are plenty of other clear examples of self-initiated self-repair; the following is only a small selection (note that we get immediate (e.g. [276]) as well as delayed (e.g. [279]) repairs in this category):

(276)   A: *and* <u>*/this one `here*</u> *# .* <u>*this /`gay one*</u> *# . /rather `grows
        'on you # (S.1.8.57.9)*

(277)   B: *(...) . he's a/bout fifty five per cent popular .
        'through"`'out # .* <u>*the /`country*</u> *# --- the /`'whole
        # .* <u>*of A/`merica # - or /half of A`merica # from
        the /((Lakes)) to the (("Canal))*</u> *# --- (S.2.1.b6.2)*

(278)   B: (...) /and 'then `'_next year_ # - _next /`real year_ # _not_
         _aca/`demic year_ # /I shall go 'back to East `Africa # -
         for an/other 'year # (...) (S.2.4.a28.7)

(279)   C: /one of '_our set `books_ was a 'Plautus # */rather a*
         B: *m*
         C: `tender 'one # -- I /mean _the `Latin `set book((s))_ #
         B: ah (S.2.5.a56.3)

(280)   A: (...) /what they've 'done # /is I `think # - you /`know # .
         /several `thousand . [/of _the `book_ #] # . _this /`paper-_
         back # . but only three hundred . of the cassettes -
         (...) (S.3.2.c17.8)

(281)   A: for example # _that [∂:m] -- [∂] "/`Tower_ #
         the "/`Mill'bank . *'tower #*
         b: *I was thinking* of that one (S.4.4.46.7)

(282)   A: (...) . /plastering _the 'thing((s))_ with a `sponge # . _this_
         /great ((bunch)) of `stamps # . (...) (S.4.6.a63.5)

(283)   A: (...) . [∂] /when ‾one # is /looking at [∂m] . _the way_
         in 'which 'one - _[thi] /tech"‗niques_ # . by /which
         one - `'analyses # . (...) S.6.1.b4.10)

(284)   A: [∂:m] - /I'm 'mending _the 'contract_ # _the /`draft_ #
         I've been /sitting on the 'draft `contract 'all this
         'time # (...) (S.8.3.h11.6)

(285)   D: (...) - /`Pete # [∂:] . /has /Pete [`'Murdoch has] given
         me a `'letter # . (...) (S.9.2.L44.3)

One instance is interactionally interesting, in that an attempt is made
by the hearer at other-correction (despite the fact that self-initiation
has already started):

(286)   D: we've /got to get 'down to the "`root [_of the dis/`ease_ #]
         # [th] _the dis/ease that_ **Mr** _the dis/ease that_ 'Mr
         M: **the dis/ease** of `hunting # .

D: *'Moor is "`suffering 'from* # - (...) (S.5.6.46.6)

As we have already seen in previous chapters, and as we will also see further on in this section, self-initiated, other-correcting repair is extremely rare (there is only one instance of this in our data; cf. section 9.2.4).

9.2.2. Other-initiated self-repair

Turning now towards other-initiated self-repair, the figures in (274) show that this is less frequent, as one would expect (16 instances, or 15% of the data). Let us consider one instance in detail:

(287)   A: (...) she's /been in this 'steady . [ə:m] /very . [`'really]
        `'good'job # at . / `lecturing at # . [ðm] the /`'training
        'college 'now # for - / `oh it 'must be . /ten or 'twelve
        'years #
        C: /what `training 'college # .
        A: /Rosary Mill #
        C: mhm . ah yeah (S.2.14.102.4)

The speaker here utters the referent *the training college*, which he considers to be sufficiently informative. However, it becomes clear that the hearer is not able to identify the referent precisely, as he initiates a repair, in a form which leaves no doubt that the precise trouble-spot is the exact reference of *training college* (viz. a *wh-*question). The speaker thus duly provides a more specific reference, in this case a proper name. As a final step in the repair process, a step which occurs quite regularly in other-initiated types of repair, we get a confirmation-signal by the hearer This is less frequent with self-initiated repair, for obvious reasons: it is only when the hearer himself has initiated the repair that he must feel obliged to confirm that the reparans the speaker has just uttered has been successful in leading to referential informativeness. We thus get a 4-stage process:

(288)   step 1: (A) utterance containing reparandum
        step 2: (B) initiation of repair
        step 3: (A) correction of reparandum through reparans
        step 4: (B) acknowledgment of reparans

Given the fact that this is a collaborative process, where speaker and hearer rely on feedback from each other to know whether a referential form has been informational enough, one would expect cases where no acknowledgment occurs, for the simple reason that effective repair has not been achieved from the first time. This is the case in (289) below:

(289)   C: *have you /tried the `bookcase* # -
   B: *I`bookcase* #
   C: *in /our `room* # ---
   B: *I´eh* # .
   C: *you know the /big ´glass ´fronted `bookcase* #
   B: *I´yeah #*
   C: *the* /`new one #
   B: /oh `that # (...) (S.7.1.a57.7)

In this instance, B initiates a repair of the reparandum *the bookcase*, after which C provides more information by adding a PP expressing the location of the referent. Rather than acknowledging the reparans, however, B signals that the referent is still not informational enough for him, after which C provides a second reparans, viz. *the big glass fronted bookcase*. Even this is not sufficient for the hearer, apparently, as he utters a new initiation signal, viz. *yeah*. Only after the third reparans (*the new one*) provided by the speaker does the hearer have enough information to confirm the successful repair. We thus get the following process:

(290)   step 1: (C) utterance with reparandum
   step 2: (B) 1st repair-initiation
   step 3: (C) 1st correction-attempt
   step 4: (B) 2nd repair-initiation
   step 5: (C) 2nd correction-attempt
   step 6: (B) 3rd repair-initiation
   step 7: (C) 3rd (successful) correction-attempt
   step 8: (B) acknowledgment of referential form

Such a process could, in principle, go on for a very long time, until successful reference is established. In practice, however, since speaker and hearer can be expected to be co-operative, the speaker will try to give a sufficiently informational form as soon as possible.

Note, though, that this collaborative process is nicely in tune with the Economy principle: every time the speaker has to make a repair, he tries to do it as minimally as possible (while still of course being more informational than in his previous reference form), assuming that the hearer will try maximally to resolve the reference problem. There is thus a delicate balance in this process all the time between Clarity and Economy, our two pragmatic principles.

The following is an interesting, related instance of an other-initiated repair which is not resolved as typically as the schema in (291) suggests:

(291)   B: oh I told you who I saw this morning # . / `David's
            mother # - *[ə:m]
        A: */`which `David #* . **oh the [dei]**
        B: **/David** `Carter # . the /one who
        A: ((the /boy you had 'written)) the 'letter a'bout the
            `music . 'lessons #
        B: (...) /ˉm # (...) (S.4.1.7.4)

What happens here is that, after the speaker has performed the (other-initiated) self-repair, the hearer (A) still has a degree of uncertainty about the referent; however, it is apparently clear enough to make an educated guess in the form of a more specific reference form, viz. *the boy you had written the letter about the music lessons*. This reference appears to be correct, hence the confirmation (by speaker B) that unambiguous reference has been achieved. Schematically, we thus get the following:

(292)   step 1: (B) utterance with reparandum
        step 2: (A) repair-initiation
        step 3: (B) correction-attempt (reparans 1)
        step 4: (A) additional correction-attempt (reparans 2)
        step 5: (B) acknowledgment of successful repair

In effect, then, what we have is a repair which has an element of other-correction in it, since the hearer provides part of the necessary referential information himself. Since the speaker provides the first reparandum, however, the repair is still mainly self-correcting.

There are a number of instances which also have an element of other-correction, but in a different sense, viz. that the hearer tries to both initiate and carry out the repair right away. The fact that this attempt at other-correction is unsuccessful, however, leads the speaker to self-correct, which means that we are dealing with other-initiated self-repair. An example:

(293)   B: /I enjoyed . I /still re`member # /that [`first 'arts 'thing
                   I did] `last 'year #
             A: it was /[thi: ?ǝm ?ǝm] the `Kenwood 'one # /`wasn't it #
             B: /`no # it was the /one be`fore 'that # (...) S.9.1.L31.4)

In this instance, the reparandum *that first arts thing* is in need of repair, a repair which is attempted by the hearer by way of *the Kenwood one*. This, however, turns out to be an unsuccessful repair; the speaker thus provides a more successful reparans, viz. *the one before that*. Schematically, we get the following (see also chapter 3):

(294)   step 1: (B)   utterance with reparandum
             step 2: (A)   repair-initiation
                                    +attempt to provide reparans
             step 3: (B)   rejection of A-reparans
                                    +successful 2nd reparans

Some other examples of this kind of self-repair with other-correcting attempt:

(295)   B: (...) -- . ((and I)) /had a con'ditional `witness
                   'summons # to /enter this 'guy's `trial #
                   [2 TUs intervening]
             A: m
             c: in Bristol . *. oh the other one . that's not it*
             B: */`no # this is an/`other 'guy # a /`London* 'guy #
                   (S.2.13.35.7)

(296)   B: un/less `these 'people [ǝ:] -- [ǝ:] /[degǝ`ma] # .
             A: are /these [thi:] 'dreaded I`talians #
             B: /`no no `no #
             A: *((al))/`right # .*
             B: *((this is))* /Gordon `Davies
             A: well (...) (S.8.4.c11.3)

(297)   B: *that `green is /not `bad # / `is it # that `landscape #*
         A: *what the bright one - *((it's))**
         B: *yes # *well it's* /not very `bright # /no I `meant
              the **second `one a`long #***
         A: ***oh that one over there***
         B: *yes - (...) (S.1.8.7.7)*

In one instance, the reparans is, as it were, constructed jointly
between speaker and hearer (most of it, though, is self-correcting):

(298)   A: *(...) /do you re'member 'that place in Tehe'ran # -
              *that place**
         D: **/ `oh [?] #\* the - /place that `sold*
         A: */ `bulls' balls # on /on sort of on *ke/babs* with
              to `matoes #*
         D: **/ `skewers #\* - / `yes #*
         A: *((you must remember that)) (S.4.6.b26.1)*

The remainder of our other-initiated, self-correcting data are more
straightforward, in that they follow the schema outlined in (288).

9.2.3. Other-initiated other-repair

Next, we will pay attention to other-initiated other-repair, which is
slightly less frequent than the previous type (11 instances, or 10% of
the data). This means that, when a repair is other-initiated (27
instances), the reparandum has a slightly higher chance (59%) of
being corrected by the speaker than by the hearer (41%). However,
one has to take into account that in some cases of other-initiated self-
repair, the hearer makes a first (unsuccessful) attempt at correction,
as we have seen above.

A straightforward example of this type of repair, which we will
discuss in some detail, is (299):

(299)   A: */ `well # . /that young gentleman from - ((the "`Park #)) .*
         B: */Joe /Joe `Wright you `mean # -- *(-- laughs)**
         A: **yes . yes* (S.1.1.49.9)*

In this instance, the hearer not only initiates repair of the reparandum *that young gentleman,* but straightaway produces a reparans, *Joe Wright,* which turns out to be the correct reference. Since the hearer, when providing the reparans, cannot be sure that he has made the right assumptions, it is essential that the speaker confirms the reparans, which happens here in the third turn. We thus argue the confirmation-move to be a vital ingredient of this repair type, so that we get the following schema (see also chapter 7):

(300)   step 1: (A) utterance with reparandum
          step 2: (B) repair-initiation + correction
          step 3: (A) confirmation of reparans provided by hearer

Naturally, in some cases, the reparans provided by the hearer will be wrong, in which case we get a self-correction sequence as represented in (294) above.

Let us now provide some more exemplification of this repair type, all following the pattern outlined in (300):

(301)   A: (...) -- /well /[w] [ə:] /what shall we do about [ə]
              `this boy then # --
          B: Du/`veen # .
          A: /`m #
          B: well (...) (S.1.2.a16.10)

(302)   B: (...) be/cause the only other - commercially available .
              'Old English 'thing I `know # /is that `record # .
          A: /that's [thi:] `Caedmon # .
          B: /`yeah # - (S.3.2.c28.4)

(303)   CF: (...) I /don't think there's enough `money in the
              department [to / `spend #] # .
          A: (- breathes) this is /money 'for the 'buying of `books #
          CF: /`yes # (S.3.3.42.1)

(304)   A: (...) . I /rather 'fancy going down the Loire
              [in / `spring #] # - /year after `next #
          B: /`mhm # - /year after `next #
          C: (- *---* laughs)
          B: *d'you /mean the **. `'spring 'after `this # / `yes #** -*

> A: *- **/no `next year # - /next `year # -** / `yes # /spring
>   'after* `next # (...) S.2.13.24.8)

Note that, in all these instances, the reparans provided by the hearer is indeed confirmed by the speaker, as we have claimed. Instance (304) is interesting, since the speaker first rejects the hearer-reparans provided, but then realizes it is correct anyway.

In all the above instances, the hearer provides the correct reparans; he can, however, not be sure that he has done so, unless the speaker reassures him in that respect. The hearer's uncertainty about his other-correction may show through in the way he introduces his repair, as is shown by the following instances:

(305)   B: /oh it's about _hyd`rology_ # . and / `that sort of thing # -
        C: is /that `´water #
        B: / `water # (S.2.8.b11.1)

(306)   B: (...) and _the / `´other 'paper_ # seems /rather to have
           gone to `pot # -- as /far as `´I can *make 'out #
           because /we've .*
        A: *((syll)) do you /mean _the phi`lology 'paper_ # .*
        B: / `yes # - (S.6.2.10.1)

(307)   A: and we'd /like to 'know what . the 'membership what
           _the `fee_ would `be # /for - [∂] the `gentleman # /he's .
           apparently a 'non`member # ---
        C: [∂:m] /you mean _conference `fee 'and [∂:?] `member-
          'ship_ # -
        A: [∂:m] / `yes # (...) S.8.3.e3.8)

The tentativeness of the hearer's reparans is reflected here in the fact that it is introduced in a question format.

There are two more instances of other-initiated other-repair in our database, both of which are a bit untypical. Instance (308) is special, in that it involves a kind of "delayed" repair, the real trouble-spot occurring a few turns after the reparandum (which is not really an NP) has been uttered:

(308)   A: (...) . /it's [∂m] set in . pre_Indian_ `´mutiny # .
        a: m

A: (([∂:m] to some extent)) --- the wife the son --
   ((6-7 sylls)) . king . shah . king - well you know
   the British .
a: viceroy - m --
A: [ku] ---
a: what [?] [i] *imperial India* *you mean*
A: */`yes #* im/`´perial ´India ´just be´fore ((`then #)) -
   (S.2.12.41.6)

In instance (309), the speaker starts repairing as well at a point where
other-repair has already started (note the overlap):

(309)   B: (...) . and /then . I think some time . "`Tom's had
        'something to 'do with him #
        a: who . *Tom *Walker**
        B: */Tom* `Walker # . (...) (S.2.6.62.9)

Since the speaker's reparandum confirms the one provided by the
hearer, there is no need for the speaker to acknowledge the hearer-
repair again.

9.2.4. Self-initiated other-repair

As a final type of repair, we can now turn towards self-initiated
other-repair. We have already pointed out on previous occasions that
such repair is quite rare. The reason for this is simple: if the speaker
initiates the repair himself, it is obviously more likely that he will
offer an alternative for the referential trouble-spot than that the hearer
will do so. Self-initiation thus nearly always leads to self-correction.
In fact, there is only one single instance of self-initiated, other-
correcting repair in the database:

(310)   B: /well I ((expect)) you don't `need 'cyphers # /during
        [thi:] /if by `that # you /mean people 'who
        a: *people who can decode* *. yeah*
        B: *'de`code and* 'things like 'that # you /don't need them
        during `peacetime # (S.2.3.71.3)

Even this is not a pure case, since the speaker does not only initiate the repair, but starts off providing a reparans; he is cut short, however, by the hearer.

As a final instance of NP-to-NP repair, we should mention (311) below, as it in fact forms a category in its own right:

(311)   B: [ǝm] listen # /mother's `clock # . is / `very is /running
         quarter of an 'hour # `'slow # . I've slightly moved
         it to a faster position but how do I move the hands
         does that . does that [ǝ] face # /spring 'off # .
      A: no no you look on the back . [ǝ:m] . [thǝ] if you look .
         (. coughs)
      B: the the three little brown . [th] the screw things .
      A: no no # [ǝ:] [i ǝ ǝ:m] if /you just '((turn)) /you /which
         'clock do you `mean # the *e/lectric 'one #*
      B: *the e/ `lectric #* . / `yeah #
      A: well (...) (S.7.2.d8.1)

Note, first of all, that this is is, like (308) above, an instance of a "delayed" repair. More importantly, however, (311) is *both* self- and other-correcting at the same time. Indeed, the reparandum *mother's clock* (cf. first turn) appears to be insufficiently informational, and the hearer thus initiates a repair (cf. *which clock do you mean*). The hearer then proceeds to provide a reparans (*the electric one*) at precisely the same point at which the speaker also utters (the same) reparans. Instance (311) can thus be called other-initiated, self- and other-correcting repair. This shows that the borderline between different types of repair is not always easily drawn, and that some repairs defy strict categorization.

9.3. Semantic types of NP>NP repair

9.3.1. [definite NP] > [proper name]

A first type of repair is the one in which a fully lexical, definite NP is replaced by an even more specific, informational one, viz. a proper name. There are 16 instances of this in the data; some examples:

(312)   A: / `well # . /that young gentleman from - ((the "`Park #)) .

*B: /Joe /Joe `Wright you 'mean # -- *(-- laughs)**
*A: *yes . yes* (S.1.1.49.9)*

(313)   A: (...) she's /been in this `steady . [∂:m] /very . [`'really]
               `'good 'job # at . /`lecturing at # . [∂m] the /`'training
               'college 'now # for - /'oh it 'must be . /ten or 'twelve
               'years #
         C: /what `training 'college # .
         A: /Rosary Mill #
         C: mhm . ah yeah (S.2.14.102.4)

(314)   B: (...) his /`'brother # was /one of the `nicest 'men I've
               'ever `known # /Arthur `Wallace # - (...) (S.6.7.41.2)

In the following instance, a proper name (first name) is repaired by
means of another, more specific proper name (first name + surname):

(315)   B: (...) . "`Tom's had 'something to 'do with him #
         a: who . Tom *Walker*
         B: */Tom* `Walker # . (...) (S.2.6.62.9)

There are slightly different instances of a proper name being repaired
by another, more specific proper name, for instance:

(316)   B: [? ∂ thi: thi:] the /Harvard 'people the the /Harvard 'Star
               people are okay to `'sell 'through # (...) (S.9.4.161.5)

In the next instance, finally, we get a reverse process, viz. a proper
name being repaired by a definite NP:

(317)   A: I /spoke to `Harry this 'morning # -
         B: /`Harry # .
         A: /`yeah # . my /`brother #
         B: [?] your `brother . and . (S.4.2.1.7)

Instance (44) is the only instance of such a reverse process in our
data.

9.3.2. [NP] > [more specific NP]

In this type, a full lexical NP is replaced by another, more informative NP. Some of the reparanda are in fact so semantically empty that they resemble pronouns in this respect; examples are *thing(s)*, *something*, *somebody* and *people* in the following instances:

(318)   B: *(...) you just get / `left [with /these `things #] # you / `know # I mean "/ `bath 'tiles # (...) (S.2.10.29.5)*

(319)   A: *(...) and you /go do 'something that you `train 'for # - an ap/ `prenticeship # /or .*
        B: */ `yeah #*
        A: *"` `something # (S.4.7.122.9)*

(320)   A: *(...) /people being `carried # /people 'being - /when I say 'people I mean `soldiers # -- /brought `in # (...) (S.6.6.37.1)*

(321)   A: *(...) /somebody 'rang [?] /one of our `students rang 'up # /wanting a - certi'fied . `statement # (...) (S.8.4.e2.2)*

These instances could thus be argued to be somewhat RD-related, as they resemble the anaphor repairs discussed in the previous chapters.

In other instances, however, the reparandum is semantically much more specified, but still not informational enough:

(322)   B: *have /you 'got a [?] - `leave 'now # - *sab/ `batical #**
        A: **/ `yes # my* /first sab'batical `term # / `ever # [ə:m] (S.1.9.18.2)*

(323)   B: */ `so # /I sup'pose `really I'm # . /carrying on *.* doing .*
        A: **(clears thoat)**
        B: *my 'own `work # my /own re`search # (...) (S.2.4.a27.2)*

(324)   A: *(...) /what they've `done # /is I `think # - you / `know # . /several `thousand . [/of the `book #] # . this / `paper-*

back # . *but only three hundred . of the cassettes -*
(...) (S.3.2.c17.8)

We will go into the information flow status of these repairs in section
9.4.

9.3.3. [NP] > [modified NP]

This is the most frequent category; over 50% of the data are of this
type. First of all, we very frequently get instances in which a bare
noun is replaced by a noun accompanied by an adjective; e.g.:

(325)   *A: oh no # - . because /I didn't 'know the ^signs the /X ray*
           ^signs # of . /`rickets you 'see # (S.2.9.22.1)

(326)   *C: (...) it's /got a 'small `cellar # . /`coal 'cellar #*
           B: /`mhm # - (S.8.2.a40.3)

(327)   *D: (...) . [∂:] in /fact that's one item on the [a`genda] the*
           do/`mestic a'genda # this /`evening # . (S.9.2.L29.8)

(328)   *A: and /if we 'have `'dinner # . /if we have 'Christmas*
           'dinner `'then # . I "/`know that # (...) (S.4.3.62.6)

(329)   *B: (...) the /`second `course # was [∂:m] . "/`goat # -*
           /`stewed goat # . [tsh] (S.4.6.b15.1)

Secondly, there are instances in which an noun gets postmodified by
a complete adnominal clause, mostly a relative clause; e.g.:

(330)   *A: [?] [∂:m] . it's /just to 'say that [?] for '[thi:] . [∂:m] [?]*
           `second 'week that you're on the '`programme # [?] the
           /one we're recording on the thirty `first # [∂:m]
           (S.9.1.L2.3)

(331)   *A: I'm "/still re"lying on "[`some of] Kalapandy's `notes # .*
           /notes I 'took of his `lectures # - (...) (S.1.6.113.4)

The postmodifier can also be a modifying PP; e.g.:

(332)   *CF: (...) I /don't think there's enough `money in the*
        department [to / `spend #] # .
        A: (- breathes) this is /money `for the 'buying of `books #
        CF: / `yes # (S.3.3.42.1)

(333)   *A: /so [∂:] - the `´man # not /not `'David # the /man in the*
        `´house # . /called the po" `lice # (S.4.7.56.8)

This list is not really exhaustive, as there are other types, usually combinations of the types mentioned here (such as a noun which gets both an adjective and a modifying clause). We will not go deeper into this, but rather look into a more interesting, funtional aspect of these repairs, viz. their status towards the E- and C-principles.

9.4. Informational status of the reparandum

Since we are dealing here with a reparans which has the form of a full lexical NP, and which is thus semantically more specific than a pronoun, it is clear that these repairs cannot be explained purely in terms of problematic recoverability, like the pronoun-to-NP repairs discussed in chapters 3 to 8.

9.4.1. Precise identification of referent

In quite a number of examples, what is at stake is precise identification of the reference of the NP being referred to. This is certainly the case in the instances in which a definite NP is repaired by means of a proper name. We have already discussed these at some length in the previous section; it will sufice here to give a few examples:

(334)   *B: /but it was a bit . the /[thi:] guy who `took the 'group #*
        A: / `'m #
        B: / `took us 'up [/ `Charles #] # (...) (S.7.3.f26.5)

(335)   *A: (...) she's /been in this `steady . [∂:m] /very . [`´really]*
        `´good 'job # at . / `lecturing at # . [∂m] the / `´training
        'college 'now # for - / `oh it 'must be . /ten or 'twelve
        ´years #

C: /what `training 'college # .
A: /_Rosary Mill_ #
C: mhm . ah yeah (S.2.14.102.4)

The point about a lot of these cases is that precise identification of the referent involved is for some reason or other of prime importance (which in a lot of other circumstances it is not: the precise identity of a personal reference often does not matter; what matters is that the NP in question is acknowledged as being referential, i.e. referring to a particular entity in the extralinguistic world). As a result, the Clarity principle becomes relatively more important, to the extent that even a full NP sometimes is not informative enough, and an even more specific proper name has to be employed.

Similarly, in some instances, in order to make more precise identification possible, the NP has to be qualified by some attributive material, such as an adjective. Again, we will only give a few additional examples, as we have already dealt with such cases in the preceding section:

(336)   A: and /_this one `here_ # . _this_ /`_gay one_ # . /rather `grows 'on you # (S.1.8.57.9)

(337)   B: I /I spent a 'year writing . [∂:m] . _the coursebook_ 'for . the linguaphone `Russian course #
        d: *which*
        B: *_the_* /`new one # - (...) (S.2.11.b144.9)

(338)   A: (...) . /is it in '_that 'cupboard `there_ 'Hilary # /on the
        B: the /`end one #
        A: /_next to the [`bottom]_ . /or [thi] . /[`no] not `'that one # .
        [thi] . [∂ ? ∂] I /think it would be [th] `that one . [`yeah #]
        # --- (...) (S.3.2.c12.3)

The two final instances are good examples of a context in which precise identification of the referent is very important, as there is a contrast between two possible *coursebooks* and *cupboards*, respectively.

9.4.2. Potential ambiguity

There are of course other reasons which may lead to the repairing of a full lexical NP by an even more specific form. The following is an example of a potentially ambiguous complex NP-reparans which thus violates the Clarity principle:

(339)   *A: I'm "/still re"lying on "[`some of] <u>Kalapandy's `notes</u> # .*
         /<u>notes I 'took of his `lectures</u> # - (...) (S.1.6.113.4)

The genitive NP in the reparans *Kalapandy's notes* is ambiguous, since it could potentially mean either *notes by Kalapandy* or *notes on Kalapandy;* from the context, it is not quite clear which one of the two might be meant by the speaker. By his repair *notes I took of his lectures*, the speaker makes clear that he in fact intends the latter.

The following is a similar case of lexical ambiguity, due to the two potential meanings of *year:*

(340)   *B: (...) - /and 'then `'next year # - <u>next /`real year # not</u>*
         <u>aca/`demic year</u> # /I shall go 'back to East `Africa # -
         for an/other 'year # (...) (S.2.4.a28.7)

In a neutral context, the word *year* would be unproblematic; however, in this context of a discussion between two academics, who are used to measuring in terms of academic years, there is potential confusion, which makes the more economical form potentially misleading.

9.4.3. Problems with lexical meaning

There are other factors which may lead to problematic referentiality. In the instance below, the lexical meaning of an NP used by the speaker is unclear, and he thus has to provide a more expanded description:

(341)   *B: /well I ((expect)) you don't `need '<u>cyphers</u> # /during*
         [thi:] /if by `that # you /mean people 'who
         *a: <u>people who can decode</u> *. yeah**

B: *'de`code and* 'things like 'that # you /don't need them
    during `peacetime # (S.2.3.71.3)

In this instance, the speaker cannot possibly have predicted that he
has been under-informative, as he could not know that the meaning
of *cyphers* is not part of the hearer's lexical knowledge. Once again,
the speaker can only make reasonable guesses about what the hearer
knows, which in this case is a matter of long-term knowledge. The
following is similar:

(342)   B: /oh it's about hyd`rology # . and /`that sort of thing # -
        C: is /that `'water #
        B: /`water # (S.2.8.b11.1)

In this exchange, the reparandum *hydrology* is clearly not in C's
lexicon, and is thus in need of clarification. The following instance,
finally, is also similar:

(343)   N: (...) - /'I advo'cate # - [ə:] . ju/'dicial - [/'beating #] # -
        /that `is # . the /use of the `cane # - [ə] /for . crimes of
        violence against the 'person # - for "/'males # . /up to
        the age of 'seventeen years # - and the /'birch # .
        "/`over seventeen years # (...) (S.5.3.9.10)

In this context (a House of Commons debate), the precise definition
of the NP referred to is very important, and might not be clear to the
hearers, so it is clarified in more explicit terms.

9.4.4. Problematic recoverability

Some instances do appear comparable to the instances of PRO-to-NP
repair discussed earlier. In the example presented below, we have a
NP which is semantically very general, and thus almost tantamount
to a pronoun; as a result, there is interference as far as the possible
antecedent is concerned:

(344)   A: /so [ə:] - the `'man # not /not `'David # the /man in the
        `'house # . /called the po"'lice # (S.4.7.56.8)

The reparans *the man* could refer to two possible referents in the previous context viz. *David* and *the man in the house*. There is thus a need for repair which is based on the problematic recoverability status of the semantically general reparandum-NP.

There are several other examples of a pronoun-like semantically general NP being repaired by means of a more specific one:

(345)   A: (...) /people_ being `carried # /people 'being - /when I say 'people I mean `soldiers_ # -- /brought `in # (...) (S.6.6.37.1)

(346)   B: (...) you just get /`left [with /these_ `things_ #] # you /`know # I mean "/`bath_ 'tiles_ # (...) (S.2.10.29.5)

In the following example, the pronominal *this* in the reparans is inferable from the context, and thus has a problematic recoverability status:

(347)   K: /well . I think the answer to this_ `question # . [ǝm] the_ /question_ `put # . /can the gene-alogist_ # . /help the_ psychologist_ # . /help the geneticist # . is /very much `yes # . (...) (S.5.2.47.7)

In the following exchange, the reparans is inferable from the extralinguistic rather than the linguistic context:

(348)   B: that `green is /not `bad # / `is it # that_ ``landscape_ #
         A: what the bright one - *((it's))*
         B: yes # *well it's* /not very `bright # /no I 'meant the_ **second 'one a`long_ #**
         A: **oh that one over there**
         B: yes - (...) (S.1.8.7.7)

The following is also derivable from the extralinguistic context. Note that precise identification of the intended referent is very important here, so informativeness is particularly relevant:

(349)   C: have you /tried the_ `bookcase_ # -
         B: / `bookcase #
         C: in /our_ `room_ # ---

> B: / ´eh # .
> C: you know <u>the /big 'glass 'fronted `bookcase</u> #
> B: */ ´yeah #*.
> C: *<u>the*</u> / `new one #
> B: /oh `that # (...) (S.7.1.a57.7)

The following is another example of a NP which is ambiguous because of its inferability:

(350)   B: [∂m] listen # /<u>mother's `clock</u> # . is / `very is /running
                quarter of an 'hour # `´slow # . I've slightly moved
                it to a faster position but how do I move the hands
                does that . does that [∂] face # /spring ´off # .
         A: no no you look on the back . [∂:m] . [th∂] if you look .
                (. coughs)
         B: the the three little brown . [th] the screw things .
         A: no no # [∂:] [i ∂ ∂:m] if /you just '((turn)) /you /which
                'clock do you `mean # <u>the *e/lectric 'one</u> #*
         B: *the e/ `lectric #* . / ´yeah # (S.7.2.d8.1)

In this instance, the referent *mother's clock* is partly inferable through its anchoring, but since there appears to be more than one *clock* that could be a candidate for coreference, some more information is in order.

9.4.5. Emotive content

There is one "repair" in the data which is interesting, in that it does not appear to be in the same category as any of the previous ones. The reparandum does not add anything to the reparans, from an informativeness point of view, but appears to be added merely for reasons of emphasis:

(351)   A: (...) -- and he /knows <u>a `lot</u> # . <u>a / `hell of a 'lot</u> # - .
         a: (...) (S.2.9.45.4)

In this case, the speaker seems to express a degree of attitudinal involvement in what he is saying. In some respects, this is thus similar to the emotive RDs discussed in chapter 6. One could argue that the addition of *a hell of* does add some information value to the reparans, as it emphasizes the large amount of knowledge of the person referred to. We are thus dealing here with a structure which is repair-like.

9.5. Prosodic aspects of NP-to-NP repair

9.5.1. Occurrence of pauses/turns after reparandum

First of all, we will discuss the occurrence of turns and, more interestingly, pauses in between reparandum and reparans; figure are shown in Table 14.

Table 14. Occurrence of pauses/turns in NP > NP repairs (N = 108)

	entire corpus		self-initiated self-repairs	
[+ turn]	29	(26.8%)	—	—
[+ pause]	53	(49.1%)	53	(67.1%)
[- pause]	26	(24.1%)	26	(32.9%)
total	108	(100%)	79	(100%)

The 29 [+ turn] instances are in fact all the cases of other-initiated and/or other-correcting repair in the data. Some of these also have a pause between reparandum and reparans, but this is disregarded in the table. Of the self-initiated, self-correcting repairs, just over two thirds (67.1%) have a pause after the reparandum; less than one in three (32.9%) does not have one. This is in line with our findings on repair-RDs, and confirms what we have claimed there. First of all, the pause can be seen in cognitive terms, as a signal of the "error" detection by the speaker, and the reprocessing taking place; it thus indicates self-initiation of the repair. Additionally, the fact that the hearer does not take the floor at a TRP (though some repairs are immediate, i.e. not at the end of a clause, and the pause thus does not fall at an outspoken TRP) can be read by the speaker as a passive indication that a repair is in order (and thus as an element of other-initiation). This would mean we are dealing with other-prompted, self-initiated self-repair.

9.5.2. TU boundaries between reparandum and reparans

As far as the occurrence of a tone unit boundary between the two parts of the repair is concerned, we can be very brief. Table 15 shows that, in the vast majority of cases, there is such a boundary, so that the reparans (the "REF') consists of one or more independent tone units with their own nucleus/nuclei.This is once again in line with our results for self-repairs (cf. chapters 3 and 4). The fact that the reparans has its own tone group (or groups) with its own nucleus (or nuclei) is hardly surprising, given the high informational value of the reparans, which is essential in the reference-establishment process. We need not go into more detail on this matter.

Table 15. Tonality of NP-to-NP repairs (N = 108)

	absolute frequency	relative frequency
[+ tone unit boundary]	97	(89.8%)
[- tone unit boundary]	11	(10.2%
total NP-to-NP repairs	108	(100%)

9.5.3. Intonation of NP-to-NP repairs

Table 16 shows the final pitch movement before the initiating and correcting phase i.e. the last tone at the end of the reparandum sequence (pre-pause or pre-turn if pause/turn are present). This table brings out clearly that falling tones (almost 70%) are far more common than rising tones (just over 30%). Once again, this is in line with the figures for repair-RDs. The falling tone can probably be interpreted the same way, i.e. as a potential floor-yielding cue on the part of the speaker which, if not taken up, becomes a passive repair-initiation-prompt. The fall also indicates that the speaker has not planned the utterance as it is in advance (in which case he would probably have used a floor-holding rise), but repairs it after the first part has been uttered.

We will leave our discussion of prosody at this; in the next section, we will discuss repairs which have yet another format than the NP-to-NP repairs discussed so far in this chapter.

Table 16. Intonation at end of reparandum in NP-to-NP repairs

fall	68	(63%)			
rise-fall	02	(2%)	FALLING	70	(69.3%)
rise	09	(8%)			
fall-rise	18	(17%)			
fall+rise	04	(4%)	RISING	31	(30.7%)
level	—	(—)			
no tone	07	(6%)			
total	108	(100%)	TOTAL	101	(100%)

9.6. Other repair formats (X-to-X repairs)

9.6.1. Interactional types

Just as was the case with NP-to-NP repairs, we can distinguish four main interactional types of repair in the database; frequencies are as follows:

(352)   self-initiated self-repair   23   (88%)
         other-initiated self-repair   02   (8%)
         self-initiated other-repair   —   (0%)
         other-initiated other-repair   01   (4%)

By far the most common repair type is thus, once again, self-initiated, self-correcting repair; other types are very infrequent, or even absent.

Self-initiated self-repair will thus be discussed first. Let us start off by looking at an instance in some detail:

(353)   A: (...) but . "/many 'local au'thorities `'now # . are /not
         re'cruiting <u>to ca`pacity</u> # - /that is to 'say # /<u>when you
         'get . a 'school . that 'say has 'got . [ə:m] twenty
         `teachers # - [ə:] /when . (([ə?])) 'one of them 'dies.
         # /or re'tires # or /moves on # . [ə:] they'll [f] /soldier
         'on with nine`teen</u> # --- (...) (S.3.2.b5.3)

In this instance, the reparandum *to capacity* (a PP) is repaired by means of an entire complex sentence giving more information (viz.

from *when you get* up to *with nineteen*). Note the initiator *that is to say,* which occurs more than once in these kind of reformulations. Some more instances of this repair type:

(354)   A: (...) . or /are you 'being . [ðm] . /please 'don't mis-
          'under'stand me when I 'say this # . "/`over'taught #
          /that is to `say # . being /asked to at`tend # . "/more
          lectures # "/more `seminars # /more tu`'torials # than
          /you can pre`pare for # - (S.3.3.72.8)

(355)   A: (...) /what is so `fascinating 'is # your /`saying # /sorry
          fascinating to `my way of 'thinking # ((/is that)) you
          `say that # (...) (S.3.4.47.3)

Note the repair-initiators *that is to say* in (354) and *sorry* in (355).

We can now turn towards the other types of repair in the data. There are two instances of other-initiated self-repair; one of them is (356) below:

(356)   A: well /we're going to 'France on the six`'teenth `too # but
          /we're going 'to the "`south of 'France you *see #*
          B: *six*/teenth of `what #
          A: [ð] Sep"`tember # . [ð ð ð] /`August # /`August #
          /`August # I'm /talking about `August # /`not
          Sep'tember # (S.8.4.c8.9)

The hearer here initiates the repair by way of a *wh*-question word; he does not attempt to provide a reparans himself.

Other-initiated other-repair is represented by one single instance in our data, viz. (357) below:

(357)   D: *it's the /`Monkish ((2 sylls))*
          A: */`yeah # .* you 'don't 'mean the . Eng'lish of `'Monk-
          land # . you /mean Monkish . to . `English #
          D: that's ((it)) (...) (S.9.2.L51.7)

This instance is in fact hard to interpret, but it seems reasonable to assume that A's *Monkish to English* is a reparans for *Monkish ((2 sylls))* in D's turn, which is thus the reparandum. Note that the speaker confirms the reparans in the third turn, which again lends support to our claim that this acknowledgent is an essential interactional step in other-correcting repairs.

As regards self-initiated other-repairs, finally, we can be very brief, as there is not a single instance of this in our corpus. Given the very low frequency of this repair type in our other data (for reasons described earlier), this is hardly surprising.

9.6.2. Syntactic and semantic types

Since the repairs discussed in this section are a heterogeneous amalgam of many formal categories, it makes sense to investigate more closely exactly which categories appear as both reparans and reparandum. The most frequent type of repair is that through which a noun (NP or PP) is replaced by an entire clause, as in (358) and (359):

(358)   W: (...) - /they dis-covered # - that in the ma/jority of cases exactly _the re`verse_ happened # /that is _there's a rather "`greater tendency for people to commit crimes a´gain_ # - / `after they'd been ´flogged # than /when _they `hadn't_ # (S.5.3.19.6)

(359)   K: (...) and /I think that the Browning quotation is right ^too # . /for _that `reason_ # . _that . we / `must_ # . _[ə] / `grow with the times_ # . '/ `learn to grow old # (...) (S.5.2.25.10)

In (358), the reparans is an independent clause, in (359) it is a dependent clause. Instance (353) above also belongs in this category.

In one instance, the reverse happens, i.e. a clause is repaired by means of two nouns (the nouns being more informational):

(360)   M: (...) mathematics - and . [ə:] - what . heraldry . and for that matter theology give to people . is colour # . and /something out`side # . /_what . an `animal ´needs_ # that's to say . /_-food_ # . /_-rest_ # - (...) (S.5.2.5.3)

In two other instances, we get a clause which is repaired by way of another clause; an example:

(361)   *D: (...) in `some of / `some of these situations # <u>the /actual</u>*
         <u>'meanings of the 'words</u> are `shifting # . /that's to say
         <u>when he says `planning # - and the /ordinary 'bloke</u>
         <u>on the Labour party 'floor says `planning # . they're</u>
         <u>/using the same ``'words # but they're /talking a'bout</u>
         <u>'different `things</u> # (...) (S.5.7.23.7)

Note the repair-initiator *that's to say* in this instance and in the
previous one.
    The remainder of the data is a heterogeneous collection,
comprising repairs of an adjective by means of another, more
informative adjective, a repair of a VP by means of another VP, and a
repair of a pronoun by means of another (reflexive) pronoun. The
following is a short summary of virtually all the formal combinations
of reparandum and reparans occurring in our database (26 instances):

(362)   *Reparandum*   —   *Reparans*
         NP (or PP)   —   clausal
         clausal   —   NP
         clausal   —   clausal
         adjective   —   adjective
         VP   —   VP

Other possibilities do not occur in our data, although, theoretically,
other combinations should be possible.

9.3.3. Prosodic aspects of X-to-X repairs

We will have a brief look at two prosodic features here: the
occurrence of pauses and/or turns between reparandum and reparans,
and the final pitch movement before the repair-initiation. First of all,
as far as the occurrence of pauses and turns is concerned, we get the
following frequencies for X-to-X repairs:

(363)   [+ turn]   4   (16%)
         [+ pause]   14   (54%)
         [- pause]   8   (30%)

The turns, of course, reflect other-initiation of repair (apart from one instance where the intervening turn is of a different nature). In self-initiated repairs, pauses are quite frequent (14 out of 22, or 64%). As we have argued before, the pause probably reflects the reprocessing being done by the speaker. In addition, the fact that the hearer does not take the floor and allows the pause might be taken by the speaker as a tacit prompt that a repair is in order (although it must be pointed out that some of the pauses are utterance-internal, and thus not located at a particularly strong TRP).

As far as the intonation —i.e. the final tone preceding initiation of the repair— is concerned, we get the following figures:

(364)   fall   14   (54%)
         rise-fall   1   (4%)   FALLING: 15 (62.5%)
         rise   3   (11%)
         fall-rise   3   (11%)   RISING: 8 (33.3%)
         fall+rise   2   (8%)
         level   1   (4%)   LEVEL: 1 (4.2%)
         no tone   2   (8%)

The majority of reparanda thus ends in a fall. In all, 62.5% (15 instances out of 24) of the repairs have a falling tone before repair-initiation, while 37.5% (9 out of 24) have a rising (or level) tone. This again indicates that the speaker first regards the utterance as "complete", and only afterwards realizes that a repair is in order. The fact that the hearer does not take advantage of the turn-yielding cue (the falling tone) may then serve as an additional repair-prompt (although it must once again be pointed out that this tone does not always occur at an outspoken TRP, some of the repairs being utterance-internal).

On the whole, we can conclude that the prosody of X-to-X repairs is very much in line with our findings for other types of referential repair.

9.7. Conclusion

In this chapter, we have attempted to show that the pragmatic principles of Economy and Clarity have a domain of applicability which is more general than that of the discourse anaphora phenomena discussed in earler chapters. To that end, we have had a look at instances in which a full NP is repaired by means of another full NP, and have found that these repairs, too, are due to the tension between the two pragmatic principles.

Another thing emerging from the data in this chapter is that the process of reference is once again established to be a collaborative process depending crucially on speaker-hearer interaction. This confirms not only the findings in earlier chapters, but also the findings on referent-introduction in Geluykens (1988b, 1992, 1993; see also Clark—Wilkes-Gibbs 1986).

This chapter also concludes our empirical analysis of informativeness repairs. In the following chapter, we will draw some general conclusions from our analyses.

Chapter 10

General conclusion

10.1. Clarity, Economy, and Collaboration

Probably the most important finding emerging from the empirical analysis in chapters 3 to 8 is the fact that the two pragmatic principles we have outlined in chapter 2, the Economy Principle and the Clarity Principle, are shown to have general applicability to the phenomenon of discourse anaphora. Time and again, it was shown that there is indeed a tension present between the two principles, a tension which gives rise to the repair phenomena discussed in previous chapters. We can conclude, then, that there is empirical evidence for the existence of these two opposing pragmatic forces operating in conversational discourse. The fact that the clash between Clarity (probably originating in the necessity to communicate in a non-ambiguous manner) and Economy (probably originating in a kind of "principle of least effort"; cf. Zipf 1949) constantly gives rise to repairs implies that the speaker has to tread a narrow line to keep the balance between the two principles when referring to entities. We thus hope to have shown here that principles originating in Grice's (1975) theory of conversational co-operation can be used as explanatory parameters for the analysis of naturally occurring discourse.

Another important, and related, conclusion that can be drawn from our analysis is that the process of referent-tracking, i.e. the computation of coreference links between subsequent mentions of the same referential item, is indeed a collaborative process which relies on speaker-hearer co-operation. Indeed, the repair mechanisms investigated here show that the speaker relies on constant hearer-feedback for the establishment of successful coreference links between different mentions of the same referent. This is shown not only by the instances of other-initiated repair discussed in chapters 3 and 7, but also by the self-initiated repairs discussed in chapter 4, for, as we have noted, there may be an element of other-initiation present in the latter type of repair as well (reflected in the pause between reparandum and reparans). This collaborative dimension was also noted in the process of referent-introduction in conversation (see Geluykens 1988b, 1992, 1993).

We should mention one more general conclusion that can be drawn from our analysis. From our discussion, it has emerged that the classification into four interactional types of repair set up by Schegloff—Jefferson—Sacks (1977) is perhaps open to refinement. Some of our data have shown that not all repairs fall neatly into one of the four main categories, but are rather hybrid forms of repair.

10.2. Information flow in conversation

As regards the analysis of how the information flow in conversational discourse operates, several conclusions can be drawn. First of all, we hope to have shown that the concept of Recoverability, as characterized in chapter 2, is a valuable, operational alternative for DA concepts such as "givenness". In our empirical analysis, it was shown that the notion of recoverability can be usefully employed for dealing with the status of referential expressions with regard to the preceding discourse context.

Secondly, we have provided evidence that the concept of recoverability is a complex, scalar notion, which in its turn can be broken down into the primary notions of inferability, referential distance, and interference. We have shown that the problematic recoverability status of the anaphors discussed in this study is the result of one of these three factors, or any combination of them. Referents can first of all be Inferable, which means that their antecedent is not explicitly present in the preceding discourse context, but can only be retrieved indirectly, through inferential linking; in many cases, this linking is by virtue of the referent belonging to the same frame or scenario as a previously mentioned element, but inferability can also be due to other factors. Secondly, referents can be Distant, which means that the antecedent is so far removed in the context that recoverability becomes a problem. It is important to realize that this is not to be understood in purely linear terms: it is not just the quantity of intervening material which determines a referent's recoverability, but also, and probably more importantly, the nature of the discourse intervening between anaphor and antecedent. Thirdly, even if a referent is inherently recoverable, in that it is present in the immediately preceding context, there may still be problems due to Interference, i.e. the presence in that context of other plausible candidates for coreference.

Finally, it was argued throughout this study that information flow in conversation is not a strictly linear phenomenon, and that a purely quantitative, linear description is inadequate.

10.3. Syntactic form and discourse function

This study has partly dealt with the intersection of a formal and functional realm, the functional dimension being the starting-point and main centre of our discussion. We have already mentioned that the formal dimension (i.e. the RD phenomenon) is prototypically organized (cf. infra); this is also, albeit to a lesser extent true for the functional one (i.e. repair), in that there are phenomena which are repair-related, and in which it is difficult to draw a boundary between what can still be considered to be repair and what cannot (cf. the question-RDs in chapter 6). The cross-section between the formal and functional realms can be represented diagramatically (cf. figure 1 on page 195), the inner sections representing prototypical instances of RD and repair, respectively, the outer ones encompassing peripheral cases (keeping in mind that the boundary between the two is fuzzy).

Section 1 represents the core of the form-function correlation (and also the core of chapters 3 to 6); it represents those repair phenomena which are realized as RD (or, put differently, those RDs which function as repair). The fact that certain cases are hard to categorize proves the point that RD defies a strict categorial approach, and is instead prototypically organized.

Section 2 represents RDs which are repair-related, i.e. have a function which bears some resemblance to repair, but which cannot be identified with repair. The question-RDs discussed in the second part of chapter 6 fall into this category. Since we are mainly concerned with repair, and only indirectly with RD, the discussion of repair-related RDs has been kept brief.

Section 5 represents RDs which are totally unrelated to repair, in that their function bears no relation whatsoever, or is not even partially reducible to, conversational repair. This category comprises the emotive RDs discussed in the second part of chapter 6; again, our discussion here has been kept to a minimum, as repair is our main concern.

Section 7, theoretically, would comprise RD-related phenomena which are totally non-repair-related; these fall outside the scope of this study altogether (although some emotive RDs could perhaps be claimed to fall into this category).

Turning towards the functional side, section 3 comprises repairs which are formally somewhat related to RD, in the sense that they also deal with the repair of a pronominal form by means of a lexical NP; some of the repairs discussed in chapters 7 and 8 would come under this heading. Also under this heading might come the peripheral RDs discussed in section 6.3.

Section 6 represents repairs which are not related to RD (but are still of the same "informativeness" type), in the sense that the item in need of repair is no longer a pronoun, but for instance also a full lexical NP. Since these repairs also merit our attention, in that they prove the same pragmatic principles to be at work, chapter 9 has dealt with them in detail.

Into section 8, finally, would fall those phenomena which are totally unrelated to RD, and which are not repairs in the strict sense either. These fall outside the scope of this study.

This discussion clearly shows that the relationship between grammatical form and discourse function is a complicated one. Although quite a sub-stantial portion of RDs are the direct reflection of conversational repair, there is no one-to-one correlation between form and function.

This study has also dealt with a specific problem which is one of the central issues in cognitive linguistics, viz. that of the fuzziness of linguistic categories, both from a functional and a formal point of view. We have attempted to show that syntactic constructions defy strict categorization, but are prototypically organized. In his recent study about categories and proto-types (Lakoff 1987), Lakoff draws several conclusions about the nature of language, among which are the following:

> Prototype-based categorization occurs in grammar. Radially structured categories exist there, and their function is to greatly reduce the arbitrariness of form-meaning correlations.

> Syntactic categories are not autonomous, nor are they completely
> predictable from semantic considerations. Instead, their central
> subcategories are predictable from semantic considerations, and their
> noncentral subcategories are motivated extensions of central
> subcategories.
> A great many syntactic properties of grammatical constructions are
> consequences of their meanings. (Lakoff 1987: 582)

The present study, apart from providing some evidence for these claims from naturally occurring conversational discourse, has tried to take this reasoning one step further, by showing that certain syntactic constructions are not only prototype-based, but cannot be properly explained, on a functional level, except by reference to their interactional discourse properties.

10.4. Final remarks and further perspectives

It is important to realize the limitations of this study, as the rather broad title would suggest that this study is an attempt at a comprehensive account of anaphora in discourse. Naturally, this is not the case. We should point out that we have only dealt with a small, specific area of anaphora, viz. the factors determining the choice between a pronoun and a full NP in contexts where this is not governed by syntactic constraints. Furthermore, we have only dealt with one type of discourse, viz. spontaneous conversation, and our analysis has been restricted to English. It would thus be worthwhile to look at anaphora from a broader (but also interactional) perspective (see Fox 1987).

As far as the problem of referent-establishment and referent-tracking in conversation is concerned, it would also make sense to take a slightly broader perspective, and to see how referents, in whatever form, are introduced, get employed as possible discourse topics, and disappear from the discourse scene. We have in fact already made a start with such a broader study on referent-introduction (see Geluykens 1993).

Finally, it would be interesting to investigate the relationship between discourse function and syntactic form from a more general perspective. RD is only one of the many syntactic constructions of English; it would probably be worthwhile to look at other constructions from a functional perspective. We have already done this to some extent for cleft sentences (Geluykens 1984, 1988a, 1991) and for Left-dislocation (Geluykens 1989, 1986b, 1989c, 1989d, 1992), but other constructions should lend themselves to a similar approach.

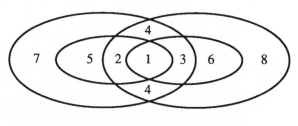

RIGHT-DISLOCATION   REPAIR

section 1: prototypical RDs functioning as repairs
section 2: prototypical RDs with repair-related function
section 3: peripheral RDs functioning as repair
section 4: peripheral RDs with repair-related function
section 5: prototypical RDs not functioning as repair
section 6: instances of repair without RD format
section 7: peripheral RDs not functioning as repair
section 8: instances of repair-related phenomena without RD format

Figure 1. Cross-section of functional and formal dimensions

References

Atlas, Jay—Stephen C. Levinson
    1981   "It-clefts, informativeness, and logical form", in: P. Cole (ed.), *Radical pragmatics*. New York: Academic Press.

Bolinger, Dwight L.
    1951   "Intonation: Levels vs. configurations", *Word* 7: 199-210.
    1982   "Intonation and its parts", *Language* 58: 503-533.
    1986   *Intonation and its parts: Melody in spoken English.* Stanford: Stanford University Press.

Brazil, David
    1975   *Discourse intonation.* University of Birmingham: Department of English.
    1978   *Discourse intonation II.* University of Birmingham: Department of English.

Brown, Gillian—Karen L. Currie—Joanne Kenworthy
    1980   *Questions of intonation.* London: Croom Helm.

Brown, Gillian—George Yule
    1983   *Discourse analysis.* Cambridge: Cambridge University Press.

Chafe, Wallace L.
    1976   "Givenness, contrastiveness, definiteness, subjects, topics, and point of view", in: C.N. Li (ed.), *Subject and topic.* New York: Academic Press, 21-55.
    1987   "Cognitive constraints on information flow", in: R.S. Tomlin (ed.), *Coherence and grounding in discourse.* Amsterdam: John Benjamins, 21-55.

Clark, Herbert H.—Susan Haviland
    1977   "Comprehension and the given-new contrast", in: R. Freedle (ed.), *Discourse production and comprehension.* Hillsdale, N.J.: Lawrence Erlbaum Associates, 1-40.

Clark, Herbert H.—C.R. Marshall
    1981   "Definite reference and mutual knowledge", in: A.K. Joshi—B.L. Webber—I.A. Sag (eds.), *Elements of discourse understanding.* Cambridge: Cambridge University Press.

Clark, Herbert H.—Deanna Wilkes-Gibbs
    1986   "Referring as a collaborative process", *Cognition* 22: 1-39.
Creider, Chet A.
    1979   "On the explanation of transformations", in: T. Givón (ed.), *Discourse and syntax.* (Syntax and semantics 12.) New York: Academic Press, 3-21.
Cruttenden, Alan
    1981   "Falls and rises: Meanings and universals", *Journal of Linguistics* 17: 77-99.
    1986   *Intonation.* Cambridge: Cambridge University Press.
Crystal, David
    1969   *Prosodic systems and intonation in English.* Cambridge: Cambridge University Press.
    1972   "The intonation system of English", in: D.L. Bolinger (ed.), *Intonation.* Harmondsworth: Penguin, 110-135.
    1975   *The English tone of voice.* London: Edward Arnold.
    1980   "Neglected grammatical factors in conversational English", in: S. Greenbaum—G. Leech—J. Svartvik (eds.), *Studies in English Linguistics.* London: Longman, 153-166.
Crystal, David—Randolph Quirk
    1964   *Systems of prosodic and paralinguistic features in English.* The Hague: Mouton.
Cutler, Anne—Mark Pearson
    1986   "On the analysis of prosodic turn-taking cues", in: C. Johns-Lewis (ed.), *Intonation and discourse.* London: Croom Helm, 139-155.
Dik, Simon C.
    1978   *Functional Grammar.* Amsterdam: North Holland.
Fillmore, Charles H.
    1975   "An alternative to checklist theories of meaning", *Proceedings of the first annual meeting of the Berkeley Linguistic Society:* 123-131.
Firbas, Jan
    1964   "On defining the theme in Functional Sentence Perspective", *Travaux Linguistiques de Prague* 1: 267-280.
    1965   "A note on transition proper in Functional Sentence Analysis", *Philologica Pragensia* 8: 170-176.
    1966   "Non-thematic subjects in Contemporary English", *Travaux Linguistiques de Prague* 2: 239-256.

Fox, Barbara A.
1987   *Discourse structure and anaphora: Written and convers-
              ational English.* Cambridge: Cambridge University Press.

Geluykens, Ronald
1984   *Focus phenomena in English: An empirical investigation
              into cleft and pseudo-cleft sentences.* (Antwerp Papers in
              Linguistics 36.) Antwerp: Universitaire Instelling Antwer-
              pen (UIA).

1986a   *Questioning intonation.* (Antwerp Papers in Linguistics 48.)
              Antwerp: Universitaire Instelling Antwerpen (UIA).

1986b   "Left-dislocation as a topic-introducing device in English
              conversation", *Proceedings of the Second Pacific Linguis-
              tics Conference:* 163-172.

1987a   "Tails (right-dislocations) as a repair mechanism in English
              conversation", in: J. Nuyts—G. De Schutter (eds.), *Getting
              one's words into line: On word order and functional
              grammar.* Dordrecht: Foris. 119-129.

1987b   "Intonation and speech act type: An experimental approach
              to rising intonation in queclaratives", *Journal of Pragmatics*
              11: 483-494.

1988a   "Five types of clefting in English discourse", *Linguistics*
              26: 823-841.

1988b   "The interactional nature of referent-introduction", *Papers
              from the 24th Regional Meeting of the Chicago Linguistic
              Society (I):* 151-164.

1988c   "On the myth of rising intonation in polar questions",
              Journal of Pragmatics 12: 467-485.

1989a   "Referent-tracking and cooperation in conversation:
              Evidence from repair", *Papers from the 25th Regional
              Meeting of the Chicago Linguistic Society (II):* 65-76.

1989b   "R(a)ising questions: Question intonation revisited", *Jour-
              nal of Pragmatics* 13: 567-575.

1989c   "The syntactization of interactional processes: Some typol-
              ogical evidence", *Belgian Journal of Linguistics* 4: 91-103.

1989d   "Information structure in English conversation: A new
              approach to the given-new distinction", *Occasional Papers
              in Systemic Linguistics* 3: 129-147.

1991   Discourse functions of IT-clefts in English conversation.
              Communication and Cognition 24: 343-358.

1992   *From discourse process to grammatical construction: On left-dislocation in English.* Amsterdam: John Benjamins.

1993   Topic-introduction in English conversation. *Transactions of the Philological Society* 91: 181-214.

Geluykens, Ronald—Louis Goossens

1989   "Information flow in conversation: Cognitive and interactional aspects", *Proceedings of the Fourth Pacific Linguistics Conference:* 154-164.

Givón, Talmy (ed.)

1983   *Topic continuity in discourse: A quantitative cross-language study.* Amsterdam: John Benjamins.

Goffman, Erving

1974   *Frame analysis.* New York: Harper and Row.

Grice, H. Paul

1975   "Logic and conversation", in: P. Cole—J. Morgan (eds.), *Speech acts.* (Syntax and Semantics 3.) New York: Academic Press, 41-58.

Gussenhoven, Carlos

1984   *On the grammar and semantics of sentence accents.* Dordrecht: Foris.

Halliday, Michael A.K.

1967   "Notes on transitivity and theme in English, part 2", *Journal of Linguistics* 3: 199-244.

1968   *Intonation and grammar in British English.* The Hague: Mouton.

1985   *An introduction to functional grammar.* London: Arnold.

Hannay, Michael

1985   "Inferrability, discourse-boundedness, and sub-topics", in: A.M. Bolkestein—C. de Groot—J.L. Mackenzie (eds.), *Syntax and pragmatics in Functional Grammar.* Dordrecht: Foris, 49-63.

Haviland, Susan—Herbert H. Clark

1974   "What's new? Acquiring new information as a process in comprehension", *Journal of Verbal Learning and Verbal Behavior* 13: 512-521.

Horn, Laurence R.

1985   "Toward a taxonomy for pragmatic inference: Q-based and R-based implicature", in: D. Schiffrin (ed.), *Meaning, form and use in context.* (GURT 1984.) Washington, D.C.: Georgetown University Press, 11-42.

Jefferson, Gail
    1972   "Side sequences", in: D. Sudnow (ed.), *Studies in social interaction.* New York: Free Press, 294-338.

Kingdon, Roger
    1958   *The groundwork of English intonation.* London: Longman.

Ladd, D. Robert Jr.
    1980   *The structure of intonational meaning: Evidence from English.* Bloomington: Indiana University Press.

Lafoff, George
    1987   *Women, fire, and dangerous things: What categories reveal about the mind.* Chicago: University of Chicago Press.

Leech, Geoffrey
    1983   *Principles of Pragmatics.* London: Longman.

Levelt, Willem J.M.
    1983   "Monitoring and self-repair in speech", *Cognition* 14: 41-104.
    1989   *Speaking: From intention to articulation.* Cambridge, MA.: MIT Press.

Levinson, Stephen C.
    1983   *Pragmatics.* Cambridge: Cambridge University Press.
    1987   "Pragmatics and the grammar of anaphora: A partial pragmatic reduction of Binding and Control phenomena", *Journal of Linguistics* 23: 379-434.
    1988   "Minimization and conversational inference", in: J. Verschueren—M. Bertucelli-Papi (eds.), *The pragmatic perspective.* Amsterdam: John Benjamins, 61-129.

Moerman, Michel
    1977   "The preference for self-correction in a Tai conversational corpus", *Language* 53: 872-882.

O'Connor, J.D.—G.F. Arnold
    1961   *The intonation of colloquial English.* London: Longman.

Owen, Marion
    1982   Review of Svartvik—Quirk 1980. *Journal of Linguistics* 18: 436-442.

Prince, Ellen F.
    1979   "On the given/new distinction", *Papers from the 15th Regional Meeting of the Chicago Linguistic Society:* 267-278.
    1981   "Toward a taxonomy of given-new information", in: P. Cole (ed.), *Radical pragmatics.* New York: Academic Press, 223-255.

Quirk, Randolph—Sidney Greenbaum—Geoffrey Leech—Jan Svartvik
  1985   *A comprehensive grammar of the English language*. London: Longman.
Reinhart, Tanya
  1983   *Anaphora and semantic interpretation*. London: Croom Helm.
Ross, John R.
  1967   Constraints on variables in syntax. [Ph.D. dissertation, MIT.] (published as Ross 1986)
  1986   *Infinite Syntax!* New York: Garland.
Sacks, Harvey—Emanuel A. Schegloff—Gail Jefferson
  1974   "A simplest systematics for the organization of turn-taking in conversation", *Language* 50: 696-735.
Sanford, A.J.—Simon C. Garrod
  1981   *Understanding written language*. Chichester: Wiley.
Schegloff, Emanuel A.
  1987   "Some sources of misunderstanding in talk-in-interaction", *Linguistics* 25: 201-218.
  1979   "The relevance of repair to syntax-for-conversation", in: T. Givón (ed.), *Discourse and syntax*. (Syntax and semantics 12.) New York: Academic Press, 261-288.
Schegloff, Emanuel. A.—Gail Jefferson—Harvey Sacks
  1977   "The preference for self-correction in the organization of repair in conversation", *Language* 53: 361-382.
Svartvik, Jan—Randolph Quirk (eds.)
  1980   *A corpus of English conversation*. Lund: Gleerup.
Van Wijk, Carel H.
  1987   Speaking, writing, and sentence form: three psycholinguistic studies. [Unpublished Doctoral dissertation, Nijmegen University .]
Zipf, G.K.
  1949   *Human behavior and the principle of least effort*. Cambridge, MA.: Addison-Wesley.

Author Index